With *Indian Food Is Easy*, and its focus on simplicity and accessibility, recreating your favorite Indian meals at home has never been easier.

Growing up in a household that celebrated food, Vijaya Selvaraju was surrounded by fragrant spices and delicious meals, thanks to her mother. As she discovered her own passion for cooking, Vijaya sought to make Indian cuisine more approachable, simplifying traditional recipes for today's busy cooks without compromising on taste. By focusing on accessible ingredients—like yogurt, rice, lentils, and fresh herbs—along with smart techniques—like using a multicooker to speed up long cooking times—she shows just how simple and enjoyable creating authentic, delicious Indian dishes can be.

Indian Food Is Easy is filled with 100 easy-to-follow recipes for every night of the week. Inside you'll find:

- **Quick and Flavorful Recipes**: Whip up dishes like the 30-Minute Keema Pav and 5-Ingredient Masala Omelet that fit perfectly into your busy lifestyle.
- **Inventive Mash-Ups:** Marry Indian spices with classic comfort food with Paneer Tikka Pizza, Vegetable Korma Pot Pie, and Tandoori Fried Chicken Wings with Spicy Lime Honey.
- **Dishes for Every Occasion**: From snack-time favorites, like Crispy Onion and Jalapeño Pakodas and Curry Popcorn Shrimp, to sweet treats, like Cardamom Orange Tiramisu and 5-Ingredient Saffron Pistachio Kulfi, you'll find recipes that cater to every craving and celebration.
- **Essential Cooking Techniques**: With practical tips and techniques, master the art of making perfect basmati rice and learn a variety of ways to make simple Indian breads, like 5-ingredient Chapatis and Crispy Rava Dosas.

Vijaya's warmth and passion shine through every page of this beautiful and approachable cookbook, complemented by stunning photography and personal anecdotes. In *Indian Food Is Easy*, you'll explore a rich tapestry of flavors, blending both beloved classics and exciting new favorites.

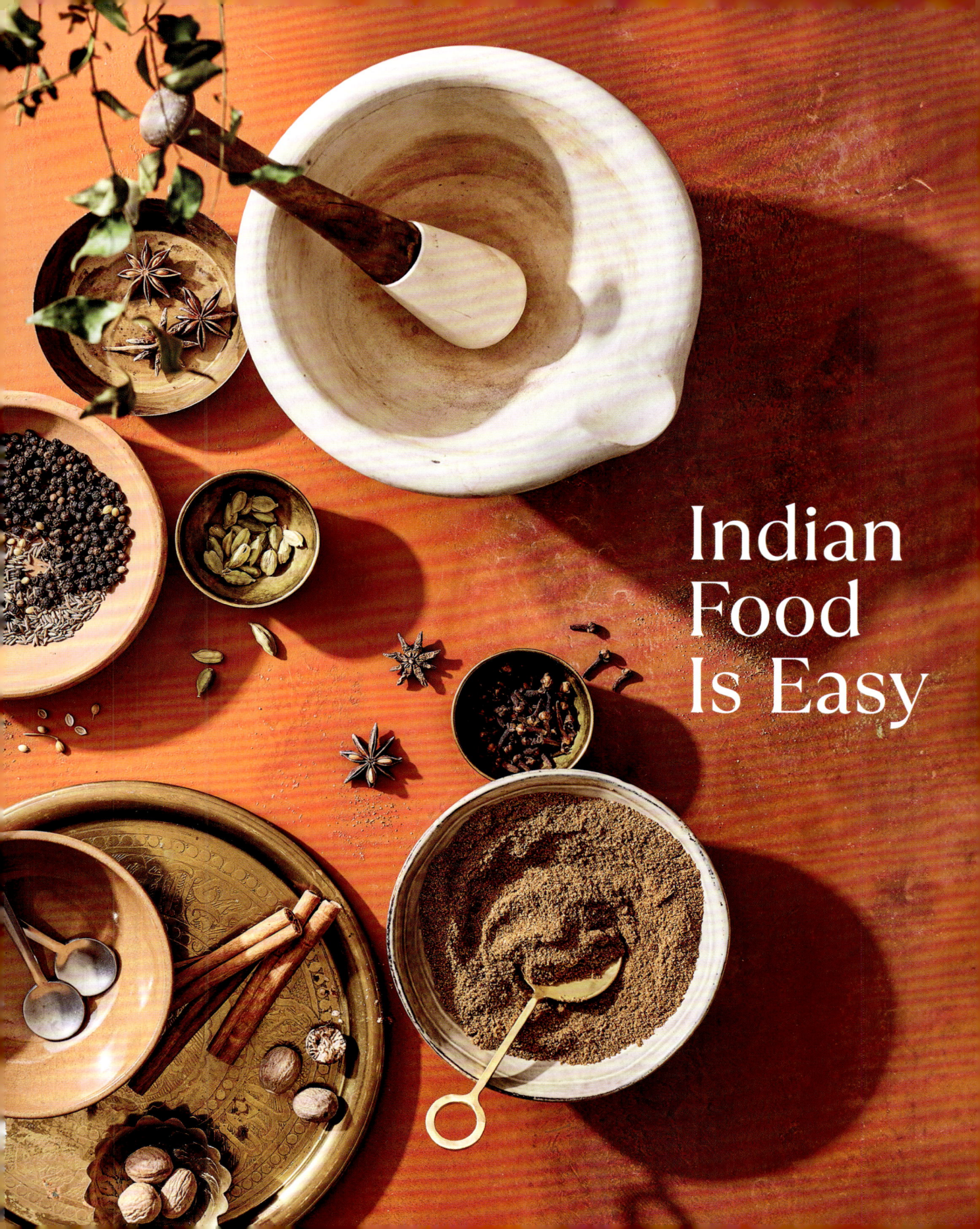

Indian
Food
Is Easy

Vijaya Selvaraju

Indian Food Is Easy

Vibrant, Comforting Recipes for Every Day of the Week

appetite
by RANDOM HOUSE

Appetite by Random House® and colophon are registered trademarks of Penguin Random House Limited.

Library and Archives Canada Cataloguing in Publication is available upon request.
ISBN: 978-0-525-61242-1
eBook ISBN: 978-0-525-61243-8

Book design by Matthew Flute
Photography by Tanya Pilgrim
Interior photography on pages v, x, 3, 4, and 240 by Memories Media
Interior photography on pages 62, 160, and 175 by Caper and Co.
Typeset by Daniella Zanchetta

Printed in China

The authorized representative in the EU for product safety and compliance is Penguin Random House Ireland, Morrison Chambers, 32 Nassau Street, Dublin D02 YH68, Ireland. https://eu-contact.penguin.ie

Published in Canada by Appetite by Random House®, a division of Penguin Random House Canada Limited.
320 Front Street West, Suite 1400
Toronto Ontario, M5V 3B6, Canada
penguinrandomhouse.ca

10 9 8 7 6 5 4 3 2 1

appetite
by RANDOM HOUSE

Penguin
Random House
Canada

*For my mom,
the best cook I know.*

*For my husband
and children,
my pillars of strength
and most supportive
taste testers.*

Contents

Rice and Grains

Breads and Dosas

Sweets

Drinks

Sauces, Spice Blends, Condiments, and Fresh Things

Introduction

Ever since I was little, I have always been surrounded by good food. My mom came from a home of well-seasoned cooks who would artfully use local ingredients—from her native Madurai, India—to put together scrumptious meals for her large family. These dishes were uncomplicated and focused on bringing out the best of each ingredient that was used.

This love of cooking has spanned generations in my family. My great-grandmother, an excellent cook herself, was once taken to a market where she encountered a man carrying a green snake. It was said that if she ran her right hand down the length of the snake that she would be an amazing cook for life, and she was! Similarly, at the tender age of seven, my mom was taken to a market where she did the same, and lo and behold, she now has a successful South Indian catering business that she has been running for more than 25 years in Toronto. Thankfully, I did not have to face this initiation. However, that family trait for preparing delicious, wholesome meals runs deep in my veins.

My earliest food memories take me back to the West African country of Cameroon where we lived until I was four years old before moving to Canada. I remember the warm paruppu sadam my mom used to make for me for lunch—a dish of creamy lentils hand-mashed together with rice with a big spoonful of nutty ghee. I also remember the fish kebabs my mom made for my second birthday laced with coriander, garlic, and hot green chilis, and my dad asking if they were too spicy for me. They were, in fact, just right.

The food we ate at home was an eclectic blend of Indian dishes with influences from my parents' travels, and this always made mealtime an adventure. From West African barbecue green chicken, to nourishing rasam, to Chinese fried rice, dinnertime was always so fun.

Moving to Canada as a young child further broadened my food education. Unlike most kids, I would watch more food television than cartoons, and by age six I was eagerly bouncing into the kitchen to help my mom make dinner. Soon enough, I was creating recipes of my own.

My passion for food continued, and despite eventually pursuing a bachelor's degree in business administration, I knew that I had to make food a permanent part of my career. I started a food blog and began sharing my recipes with my community of friends and family. That eventually evolved to sharing posts on Instagram, and one day someone happened to see my work and invited me to be on *The Marilyn Denis Show*. A couple of months later, I became one of the hosts of a national cooking show where I'd be teaching viewers how to make Indian food.

This is when I really hunkered down to study the intricacies of my mom's cooking. I learned the magic of a fragrant thalippu (hot seasoned oil), how to cook perfect rice dishes, and the specific techniques that took curries to the next level. As a way for me to document these recipes for myself, I turned to video—more specifically, YouTube— where I could create a library that I could personally refer to. I soon realized that these videos were helping many Indian food lovers around the world who were looking to recreate their favorite dishes at home.

One of the main comments I would often get from viewers was "Wow, I didn't realize that this Indian dish was so easy to make!" I've found that the number-one reason people hesitate to cook Indian food is its perceived complexity and time needed to prepare a dish. Many people feel overwhelmed by all the spices involved and think that each dish has to stew on the stove for countless hours to develop authentic flavor. To help you start navigating the world of Indian spices, I've included a Spice Library (page 6), which lists every single spice used in this book along with a description of its flavor, what dishes it can be used in, as well as substitutions in the case that you can't find it. In the Top Staple Ingredients section (page 12), I showcase 12 ingredients that I always have on hand to get an Indian meal on the table quickly. Once you become familiar with these two sections, I guarantee you will have a fantastic understanding of the base ingredients required for Indian cooking and will be raring to get in the kitchen!

As a busy woman myself, I have developed shortcuts, swaps, tips, and tricks to help get Indian meals on the table in about 30 minutes, because that is usually all the time I have. However, my goal is to always stay true to the authentic flavors without compromising on tradition. The resulting dishes in this book taste as they would in India but can be made in a fraction of the time.

Throughout *Indian Food Is Easy*, you will find a series of recipes ranging from snacks and appetizers all the way to sweets and drinks from different parts of India. In the Snacks and Appetizers chapter, you'll find Crispy Onion and Jalapeño Pakodas (page 26) and 5-Minute Masala Corn (page 32). Not only are they quick to make, but they are also big crowd pleasers!

I have developed shortcuts, swaps, tips, and tricks to help get Indian meals on the table in about 30 minutes, because that is usually all the time I have.

When I shared my chickpea curry recipe (30-Minute Amritsari Chole, page 47) from the Vegetables and Legumes chapter with my mom, she was blown away by its rich flavor profile—the greatest compliment I could ever receive! The South Indian Potato Masala (page 50) is another standout that takes the humble potato and jazzes it up with chilis, ginger, and spices.

If chicken is your thing, try The Best Butter Chicken (page 72) in the Poultry and Eggs chapter. It's the recipe my viewers consistently rave about. In the Seafood chapter, I share a simple but flavor-packed marinade for my 4-Ingredient Tamil Nadu Fish Fry (page 97) that can be used to dress up any type of fish. The 20-Minute Coconut Fish Korma (page 100) is a nod to coastal cooking and features an aromatic broth flavored with ginger, mint, and coriander. Comfort food at its best!

If you are a fan of the classics, then check out the Goan Pork Vindaloo (page 125) in the Meat chapter. While this curry is typically on the fiery side, I have tempered it so that it's not too spicy. Don't miss the 30-Minute Keema Pav (page 118), which is like an Indian sloppy joe with spiced ground lamb stuffed between buns. I could probably eat five in one sitting!

I know rice can sometimes be challenging to cook, so I have dedicated an entire chapter to it. I share my favorite way to prepare classic basmati rice so that each grain is perfect every single time. Then I take it to the next level with variations, including coconut rice and tomato rice. And if you have ever dreamed of making butter naan at home, my recipe in the Breads and Dosas section tastes exactly like the naan you get at your favorite Indian restaurant: slightly charred with a bit of chew, and all the melted butter you could dream of. Being South Indian, I am especially excited to share my dosa recipes with you. You'll love the lacy, crispy texture.

Then come the treats with sweets and drinks! The unique technique in my Classic Gulab Jamun (page 186) recipe will make them tender and custardy every single time. Sweet Lime Soda (page 206) is the one drink you can serve with just about any Indian meal. It's refreshing and effervescent, and does a great job of tempering the heat when things start to get spicy.

And because I love having fun in the kitchen, I've also included several mash-up recipes that highlight how Indian flavors can be incorporated into popular mainstream dishes (this is something I often play around with at home). Think Palak Paneer Lasagna (page 57), Curry Popcorn Shrimp (page 35), and Tandoori Fried Chicken Wings with Spicy Lime Honey (page 80)!

My goal is to help you realize that Indian food is indeed easy to prepare and can be pulled off any night of the week. You can enjoy super-authentic flavor without ever having to reach for a takeout menu. Once you start familiarizing yourself with the ingredients and techniques in this book, cooking Indian food will become more and more intuitive, allowing you to play around and create variations of recipes unique to your preferences.

It has been an absolute joy writing this book, and I can't wait for you to dig into these recipes. Enjoy!

My goal is to help you realize that Indian food is indeed easy to prepare and can be pulled off any night of the week.

Spice Library

When most people think of Indian food, the first thing that comes to mind are spices. While the laundry list can be long and intimidating, I am here to share how these spices can enhance your dishes and bring the best flavors to your meals.

Nowadays, big-box grocery stores often have an aisle dedicated to international spices where you'l be able to find pretty much everything you need. However, if you ever find yourself stuck, Indian grocery stores will always be well stocked, and many spices can be found online with just the click of a button. (I love the internet!)

While I know the list of spices I have included here is quite substantial, there is no need to buy all of them in one go. Slowly start building your spice library starting with a few basics: coriander, cumin, garam masala, Kashmiri chili powder, and turmeric. These are the spices featured most in this book.

If you end up buying your spices in larger quantities, I highly recommend freezing them in small resealable plastic bags to help maintain their freshness. Any spices you have in rotation in your pantry should be stored in airtight containers and kept away from sunlight to preserve their potency.

AMCHUR POWDER

Unlike ripe mangoes, green mangoes pack a sour punch. Once dried and pulverized into a powder, they become amchur, a delicious seasoning that adds a pop of tang to dishes like my chickpea curry (30-Minute Amritsari Chole, page 47). If you can't find it, a squeeze of lemon is a great substitute!

Black Cardamom

Asafoetida

Amchur
Powder

Anardhana
Powder

Black
Mustard
Seeds

Black Salt

Black Pepper

Carom Seeds
(Ajwain)

Cayenne Chili
Powder

Chaat
Masala

Cinnamon
Sticks

Coriander

Cloves

Cumin

Dried Red Chilis

Dried Mint

Fennel Seeds

Garam Masala

Green Cardamom

Kashmiri Chili Powder

Indian Bay Leaf

Turmeric

Star Anise

Kasoori Methi

Nigella Seeds

ANARDHANA POWDER

Fruity and sour, anardhana powder is made of pulverized dried pomegranate seeds. Similar to amchur, they add a bit of tang to Indian dishes, but can be replaced with a squeeze of lemon in a pinch.

ASAFOETIDA

Asafoetida, also known as hing, is a gum resin used in Indian cooking that is sought after for its garlicky onion flavor. As certain people's belief systems in India do not allow them to consume garlic and onion, this intense powder serves as a wonderful substitute. It is quite strong in flavor, so a little goes a long way.

BLACK CARDAMOM

Black cardamom is like green cardamom's older cousin. Its pod is almost three times the size of a green cardamom pod and is much more fibrous and tough. Used exclusively in savory dishes, black cardamom has a deep smoky flavor that works incredibly well in curries. It is typically used whole and bloomed in hot oil to help release its flavor.

BLACK MUSTARD SEEDS

Earthy, nutty, and bitter, black mustard seeds often make their appearance at the very beginning of Indian recipes to help build a base of flavor, or at the very end when they're popped in hot oil before being poured over a dish as a final seasoning.

BLACK PEPPER

Smoky and spicy, black pepper is one of the most versatile spices. It can be used whole, crushed, or ground. It is the signature flavor in my Chicken Pepper Fry (page 84). Black pepper, incidentally, pairs very well with cumin with the heat of the pepper playing off the earthiness of cumin.

BLACK SALT

Also known as kala namak, black salt is a rock salt with a funky pungent aroma. A little goes a long way, and it should never be substituted 1:1 for regular salt in a recipe, as it is used more for its aroma than for its salty profile. Black salt is featured in the popular seasoning blend chaat masala and in my Pav Bhaji recipe (page 23).

CAROM SEEDS (AJWAIN)

Though they only appear in one recipe in this book (Besan ka Cheela, page 176), carom seeds are fun to have on hand for spicing up fried dishes like pakodas and samosas. Similar in flavor to caraway seeds, carom seeds are peppery and have a slight licorice-like taste.

CAYENNE CHILI POWDER

If you're looking for a punch of heat, cayenne chili is the way to go! It is the chili powder I use most often in my cooking, registering between 30,000 and 50,000 Scoville heat units. While I provide measurements for chili powder in each recipe to accomplish a mild flavor profile, feel free to add more or less according to your taste.

CHAAT MASALA

A funky spice blend used to flavor many street food dishes, chaat masala is tangy, spicy, aromatic, and salty. It's featured in my Nacho Chaat recipe, but I also love sprinkling it generously over a bowl of chopped fruit for a fast and easy snack.

CINNAMON STICKS

Cinnamon sticks are one of the most popular whole spices used in Indian cooking. Their sweet and spicy aroma comes to life when toasted in hot oil or boiled in water or milk.

CLOVES

Universally known for their sweet and spicy flavor profile, cloves are often added to Indian dishes at the beginning of the cooking process when they are bloomed in oil. You'll know you have toasted your cloves enough when they puff up and almost triple in volume. Cloves are often bloomed in oil together with other spices like cinnamon stick, green cardamom, and Indian bay leaf.

CORIANDER

Coriander refers to the dried seed of the coriander plant. It has a gorgeous citrusy flavor and is used both coarsely and finely ground. Coriander is often partnered with turmeric and chili powder (cayenne or Kashmiri) as the base of flavor for many Indian dishes.

CUMIN

Cumin is one of my most beloved spices, and the one I reach for most often when I'm cooking Indian food. Used both in its ground and whole forms, it has a beautiful earthy flavor that works really well with other spices. Buy cumin seeds whole and grind them in small quantities in a small coffee grinder to get the freshest, most aromatic flavor.

DRIED MINT

I love dried mint because it has a beautiful floral, almost tea-like quality that adds so much dimension to dishes like my Crispy Aloo Tikki Burgers (page 30). I also like having it on hand to add a bit of pizzazz to vinaigrettes and marinades when I'm looking to switch things up a bit.

DRIED RED CHILIS

Dried red chilis are used in Indian dishes to impart a bit of smokiness and heat. They are usually toasted, either dry in a pan or with a touch of oil to bring their flavor to the surface.

FENNEL SEEDS

Used whole or ground, fennel seeds have a delicious, sweet anise-like flavor that works well in vegetarian and meat dishes. I particularly love adding them to lamb.

GARAM MASALA

Hailing from North India, garam masala is the revered spice blend that is used generously in several of the recipes you will see in this book. Every family has their own variation, and I've included mine in the Sauces, Spice Blends, Condiments, and Fresh Things chapter (page 238). Aromatic with the flavors of coriander, cumin, cardamom, cloves, cinnamon, nutmeg, star anise, and black peppercorns, it's best when you grind your own at home. It makes all the difference!

GREEN CARDAMOM
Green cardamom pods are tough and fibrous on the outside, while holding tiny fragrant black seeds on the inside. Sweet and almost perfume-like, they can be used whole to subtly impart their flavor to dishes, or finely ground for more intensity. I particularly love green cardamom in desserts like Tapioca Payasam (page 181) and my 20-Minute Badam Halwa (page 199).

INDIAN BAY LEAF
One leaf is usually all it takes to impart the fragrant cinnamon-like aroma of Indian bay. While they can sometimes be found fresh, I find it much more practical to have the dried leaves on hand. I love throwing a leaf into boiling water before preparing basmati rice—it makes it extra delicious.

KASHMIRI CHILI POWDER
If you like a hint of chili in your dishes but don't want anything too spicy, Kashmiri chili powder is for you. It has a vibrant red color and a mild sweet heat that makes it a welcome addition to Indian dishes. Feel free to use Kashmiri chili anywhere you see cayenne chili in this book if you're looking to tame the heat.

KASOORI METHI
If you've ever had butter chicken, then you'll have tasted the magic of kasoori methi. The dried leaves of the fenugreek plant look similar to dried oregano once crushed but carry the slightly bitter and earthy flavor of celery.

NIGELLA SEEDS
While I don't use nigella seeds, also known as kalonji, very often, they are a fun addition to your spice library if you're able to find them. These intensely oniony seeds make an appearance in my Achari Chicken Curry (page 76) and are also great pressed into the top of naan or kulcha dough before baking.

STAR ANISE
There is no mistaking star anise—its beautiful star shape is immediately recognizable. It is typically used whole and imparts an anise-like note to curries and rice dishes.

TURMERIC POWDER
Intensely yellow and known for its nutritional and medicinal qualities, this super spice is featured in many Indian dishes. Bitter, earthy, and musky, turmeric forms the base of flavor for many dishes. It is usually paired with cayenne chili powder or Kashmiri chili powder and ground coriander.

Top Staple Ingredients

Over time, I've learned to always keep certain key ingredients stocked in my pantry, fridge, and freezer so that I'm able to cook Indian food any time I want, without having to run to the grocery store.

BASMATI RICE
In India, basmati is the king of rice, known for its unique aroma and beautiful long grains. For the recipes in this book, I use white basmati rice. However, brown basmati (which still has its bran and germ intact) can be substituted. Just keep in mind that it requires a slightly longer cooking time than what is suggested in my recipes.

COCONUT
Coconuts are abundant in India, which is why they are used so often in our cuisine. The rich, creamy, and slightly sweet flavor of coconut is welcome in desserts, chutneys, curries, and other sweet and savory dishes. I like having tins of full-fat coconut milk (no sugar added) in my pantry at all times. I also have grated frozen coconut in the freezer for when I need to make a chutney quickly. However, I do prefer to buy a whole coconut, crack it in half, and grate the flesh myself when I have the time. Dried coconut unfortunately cannot be substituted for the fresh and frozen listed in my recipes as it does not have the ideal flavor required to maintain the authenticity of the dishes.

CURRY LEAVES
Pine-like in aroma and flavor, curry leaves are a one-of-a-kind ingredient that add so much dimension to Indian dishes. They can frequently be found fresh at Asian markets still attached to their branches, and can be easily stripped off.

Unfortunately, there are no substitutes for the unique flavor of curry leaves. If you are lucky enough to find them, try to use them while they are bright and green. Place any leftover leaves between paper towels and store them in the fridge.

DHAL

Dhal refers to dried lentils. There are many varieties of dhal, and because they are shelf stable, I love to keep a variety on hand in my pantry. I often use urad dhal (black gram) in my spiced tempered oil in rice dishes and chutneys, while toor dhal (pigeon peas), chana dhal (split chickpeas), moong dhal (split mung beans), and kidney beans are always on standby when I want to make a comforting bowl of creamy dhal to go with rice or chapatis. Many varieties of dhal can easily be found in the international aisle of your local grocery store. However, if you're trying to find a more obscure variety, your local Indian grocery store or shopping online are your best bet.

FRESH CORIANDER (CILANTRO)

Fresh coriander, also known as cilantro, is an absolute must in Indian cuisine. It often makes an appearance as a final garnish for curries, is ground into chutneys, and is cooked into rice dishes like biryani. To keep coriander fresh, I fill a jar halfway with cold water and place the stems in the water. I cover the leaves with a resealable plastic bag, which helps keep them from drying out, and then place the jar in the fridge. Coriander can stay fresh this way for up to a month—just be sure to change the water every week.

GARLIC/GINGER

I pair garlic and ginger together here because they very frequently go hand in hand as the foundation flavors in Indian recipes. I like having fresh bulbs of garlic on the counter at all times, and ginger stored in the freezer. (If you find that you don't use ginger often in your cooking, storing it in the freezer is a great way to preserve it.) Anytime I need garlic or ginger for a recipe, I finely grate my frozen ginger on a Microplane, and it's good to go—no need to thaw it.

GHEE

Nutty and rich, ghee is a type of clarified butter, where all the milk solids have been removed. As a result, it has a higher smoke point than butter, allowing you to cook with it at higher temperatures without the risk of it burning. While ghee can be purchased ready to go at the grocery store, it is so much more economical to make at home, and it is infinitely more delicious.

MINT

Mint is used frequently in fresh preparations like raita and chutneys as well as cooked dishes like biryani and kebabs. Mint can be stored in the same way as fresh coriander, with the stems in a jar filled halfway with water and the leaves covered with a plastic bag in the fridge.

Here's a simple recipe for ghee:

1. Place a 1 lb (450 g) block of unsalted butter in a large saucepan on medium-low heat, and melt completely.

2. Increase the heat to medium and cook for 4 to 5 minutes or until the mixture becomes foamy and starts to rise.

3. Reduce the heat to medium-low, and continue cooking until the foam starts to separate from the golden ghee underneath. Remove from the heat and allow to cool.

4. The milk solids will rest at the bottom of the pan, with the clear ghee on top. Slowly pour the ghee into a jar, discarding the milk solids, cover, and store in the fridge for up to 6 months.

PASSATA

The unsung hero of the Indian kitchen, passata is a jarred tomato sauce featuring tomatoes that have been picked at the height of their season, puréed, and strained. This is my favorite shortcut for making curries quickly, as its flavor is wonderful any time of the year (unlike fresh tomatoes) and doesn't require all the chopping, puréeing, and so on required with fresh whole tomatoes.

THAI GREEN CHILIS

The thing I love about Thai green chilis is that while they do pack a fair bit of heat, they are also super aromatic and add a gorgeous fresh bite to dishes. Since they're small, there's a lot of flexibility in how spicy you can make a dish, so add as few or as many as you like depending on your preference. To preserve Thai green chilis, I remove their stems, wrap them in paper towel, and store them in a resealable plastic bag in the fridge.

YOGURT

Yogurt is an essential part of Indian cuisine and is featured across the board in curries, sauces, drinks, and desserts. I always keep a couple of tubs in the fridge because I use it so often. Full-fat yogurt (4% milk fat or more) is best for the recipes featured in this book as it has the required richness. However, if you find yourself in a bind, a lower-fat yogurt could work in a pinch.

Snacks
and
Appetizers

Easy Mixed Vegetable Samosas

MAKES
30 SAMOSAS

2 Tbsp canola oil, plus more
for deep frying

1 Tbsp cumin seeds

1 medium onion, finely chopped

1 medium russet or Yukon gold
potato, peeled and diced
(about 2 cups)

1 small carrot, peeled and diced

½ cup water, divided

Kosher salt

½ cup frozen peas

¼ cup chopped fresh coriander
(cilantro)

¼ cup all-purpose flour

20 frozen spring roll wrapping
sheets (about 10 × 10 inches/
25 × 25 cm), thawed

½ cup Mint Coriander Chutney
(page 236), for serving

½ cup 4-Ingredient Tamarind
Chutney (page 231), for serving

These samosas are a crowd pleaser. In fact, when I was in elementary school and there was any opportunity to bring food to share, my teachers and classmates would always request them. Their crispy exterior makes them incredibly moreish, and the best part is that they're made with store-bought frozen spring roll wrappers, which fast-tracks this recipe! The filling features potatoes, carrots, and peas, which are very simply flavored with cumin seeds and fresh coriander. The contrast between the soft filling and the crunchy, crispy shell is absolutely addictive!

Heat 2 Tbsp of the oil in a frying pan on medium-high heat. Add the cumin seeds and let them toast and crackle for 15 seconds. Add the onion and sauté until it has softened, 3 to 4 minutes. Add the potato and carrot to the pan, and sauté for 2 to 3 minutes. Add ¼ cup of the water, season with salt to taste, stir, and cover with a lid. Cook for 5 minutes. Most of the water should be absorbed by the vegetables at this point.

Remove the lid from the pan and add the frozen peas. Cook for 1 minute, until the peas have warmed through. Remove the pan from the heat and stir in the fresh coriander. Allow the mixture to cool for 10 minutes.

Place the flour and the remaining ¼ cup water in a small bowl and mix to form a thick paste.

Cut the stack of thawed spring roll wrapper sheets into 3 even rectangles, about 3¼ × 10 inches (8 × 25 cm) each. From 1 rectangle, peel away 2 sheets together to form the pastry for the samosa. Store the remaining sheets under a damp cloth to prevent them from drying out.

recipe continues

Lay the pastry horizontally on a clean surface. Fold the pastry down the middle vertically to create a crease in the center. Open the pastry back up and take 1 corner of the pastry rectangle and bring it toward the crease, forming a triangle. The edge of the pastry should align with the crease. Spread the flour paste along the edge of the pastry that forms the triangle, then fold over the other corner of the pastry to form a cone.

Add 1 to 2 Tbsp of the filling to the cone. Fold over the remaining pastry to create a triangle, and seal the edges with the flour paste. Repeat with the remaining filling and samosa wrappers.

In a deep frying pan or wok, heat 3 inches (8 cm) of oil to 350°F. Fry the samosas in batches for 4 to 5 minutes, gently flipping once or twice during frying, until crispy and golden.

Drain on a paper towel. Serve hot with both chutneys.

Pav Bhaji

SERVES 4

1 medium russet or Yukon gold
  potato, peeled and diced

½ cup frozen green peas

2 cups chopped tomatoes

1 small beet, boiled, peeled,
  and grated

2 cups water, divided

2 tsp garam masala

2 tsp Kashmiri chili powder

2 tsp amchur powder
  (or juice of ½ lemon)

½ tsp black salt (optional)

Kosher salt

½ cup unsalted butter, divided

¼ tsp asafoetida

1 Tbsp kasoori methi

1 small yellow onion, finely chopped

½ green pepper, seeded and
  finely chopped

8 small brioche buns, sliced
  in half horizontally

½ cup finely chopped red onion

¼ cup finely chopped fresh
  coriander (cilantro)

Pav bhaji is a dish of mixed vegetables mashed together in a large frying pan with spices and butter until creamy and unctuous. This is the ideal recipe to use up any vegetables you have hiding in the corner of your crisper, as they will melt into this curry beautifully. I love eating this dish during the fall and winter, as it's hearty and heartwarming. Get those hot buttered buns ready for scooping!

Bring a medium pot of water to a rapid boil. Add the potato and cook until very tender, 15 to 20 minutes. Add the frozen green peas and boil for an additional 2 minutes. Drain and set aside.

To a large frying pan, add the tomatoes, beet, and 1 cup of the water. Bring to a simmer, and cook for 5 minutes to soften the tomatoes. Add the cooked potatoes and peas, garam masala, chili powder, amchur powder, black salt, and salt to taste. Mash with a potato masher, mixing and blending all the vegetables together. Once somewhat homogeneous and creamy in texture, transfer the mashed vegetables to a bowl.

Heat the same frying pan on medium heat and add ¼ cup of the butter. Once hot, sprinkle in the asafoetida and kasoori methi, stirring for 10 seconds to warm through. Add the yellow onion and green pepper. Sauté for 3 to 4 minutes or until the onion is translucent and soft.

Return the mashed vegetables to the pan with the remaining 1 cup of water. Stir together and bring to a simmer. Cook until the mixture coats the back of a spoon. It should be slightly thick, but still pourable. Add more water if necessary to achieve this texture.

recipe continues

Heat a large frying pan on medium heat. Add the remaining ¼ cup of butter to the pan and let it melt. Place the split brioche buns in the pan, and toast for 1 minute on each side or until golden brown.

To serve, spoon the mashed vegetable curry into a shallow bowl and garnish with the red onion, fresh coriander, and a knob of butter if desired. Serve with the toasted brioche buns for dipping and scooping.

Crispy Onion and Jalapeño Pakodas

SERVES 4

2 medium yellow onions, peeled and thinly sliced

2 jalapeño peppers, sliced into thin rings (see note)

¼ cup chopped fresh coriander (cilantro)

1 cup chickpea flour

2 Tbsp white rice flour

1 tsp kosher salt

⅓ to ½ cup water

Canola oil, for deep frying

½ cup Mint Coriander Chutney (page 236), for serving

These fried lacy fritters are synonymous with Indian cuisine and come in many variations. For this version, I like the contrasting flavors of the sweet onion and spicy jalapeño. They're crispy and crunchy, and they're perfect served with a tall cold drink like my Sweet Lime Soda (page 206).

Place the onions, jalapeños, fresh coriander, chickpea flour, rice flour, and salt in a large bowl. Toss to coat the vegetables in the flour. Allow to sit for 5 minutes to draw out any moisture.

Slowly dribble in ⅓ cup of water, stirring, until a sticky paste forms around the vegetables. The vegetables should stick together when you grab a pinch of the batter. If not, continue adding water 1 Tbsp at a time, until the mixture is slightly sticky.

In a wok or deep pot, heat 3 inches (8 cm) of oil to 375°F. Using 2 soup spoons, scoop up some batter and gently push it into the oil, making sure not to crowd the pan. Fry for 6 to 7 minutes, turning once or twice, until deeply golden and crunchy.

Drain on a paper towel. Serve hot with chutney.

Note: If you want to cut back on the heat, feel free to remove the seeds and white ribs of the jalapeños before slicing them.

Nacho Chaat

SERVES 4

1 large russet potato

2½ Tbsp chaat masala, divided

1½ tsp cayenne chili powder, divided

Juice of ½ lemon

Kosher salt

¾ cup plain yogurt

1 Tbsp sugar

4 cups tortilla chips

⅓ cup 4-Ingredient Tamarind Chutney (page 231)

⅓ cup Mint Coriander Chutney (page 236)

½ cup finely diced red onion

¼ cup finely diced cucumber

¼ cup pomegranate seeds

1 thinly sliced jalapeño pepper

¼ cup chopped fresh coriander (cilantro)

Bringing together two of my favorite things, nachos and chaat (an Indian snacky street food), this dish is a must when hosting game day. The tortilla chips serve as the perfect canvas for all the incredible toppings, including the chaat masala spiced potatoes, tangy tamarind chutney, and bright and juicy pomegranate seeds. Spicy, savory, creamy, sweet, crunchy, and smooth—each bite is an adventure!

Place the potato in a medium pot and cover with cold water. Bring the water to a boil and cook until the potato is fork tender. Drain the potato and allow it to cool until it's easy to handle, then peel and chop into small cubes.

To a large bowl, add the potatoes, 2 Tbsp chaat masala, 1 tsp chili powder, lemon juice, and salt to taste. Mix until the potatoes are well coated.

In a small bowl, whisk together the yogurt and sugar.

To assemble, spread the tortilla chips on a large serving plate. Distribute the spiced potatoes evenly over the chips, and top with the sweetened yogurt.

Drizzle the tamarind chutney and mint chutney overtop, and garnish with the red onion, cucumber, pomegranate seeds, jalapeño, and fresh coriander. Lastly, sprinkle on the remaining ½ Tbsp chaat masala and ½ tsp chili powder.

Crispy Aloo Tikki Burgers

SERVES 6

For the Patties

4 medium russet potatoes

Kosher salt

3 Thai green chilis, finely minced

½ Tbsp amchur powder
  (or ½ Tbsp chaat masala
  or juice of ½ lemon)

2 tsp ground coriander

2 tsp ground cumin

2 tsp dried mint

½ tsp cayenne chili powder

½ cup cornstarch

⅓ cup canola oil

For Assembly

6 burger buns

3 Tbsp melted butter

¼ cup mayonnaise

2 cups shredded iceberg lettuce

1 large tomato, thinly sliced

1 red onion, thinly sliced

1 cup Mint Coriander Chutney
  (page 236)

A good portion of the population in India are vegetarians, and it is very common to find plant-based burgers on the menus of the most popular fast-food chains. These crispy aloo tikki burgers are packed with flavor—they're slightly tangy with the addition of amchur powder, and earthy and aromatic with cumin and dried mint. Their beautiful crispy texture can be attributed to my secret ingredient, cornstarch, and will make you completely forget about the lack of meat. They are delicious served on their own or with French fries sprinkled with some cayenne chili powder and salt.

To make the patties, place the potatoes in a large pot and cover with cold water. Bring to a boil and cook until fork tender. Drain the potatoes and allow to cool until they're easy to handle, then peel.

Grate the boiled potatoes using the coarse side of a box grater. Transfer to a bowl and season with salt to taste, the chilis, amchur powder, ground coriander, ground cumin, mint, and chili powder. Gently mix by hand until well combined.

Take ⅓ to ½ cup of the potato mixture and form into a small round patty, about 2½ inches (6.5 cm) in diameter. Dip the patty into the cornstarch on both sides, then shake off any excess cornstarch.

Heat the oil in a large frying pan on medium-high heat. Once the oil is hot, add the patties, making sure not to crowd the pan. Cook for 2 to 3 minutes on each side or until golden brown and crispy. Cook in batches if necessary. Drain onto a paper towel.

To assemble, brush the burger buns with butter and toast in a frying pan until golden.

Spread some mayonnaise on the bottom bun, and top with the shredded lettuce, an aloo tikki patty, a slice of tomato, and some thin slices of onion. Spread the mint coriander chutney on the top bun and sandwich the burger together.

5-Minute Masala Corn

SERVES 6

6 ears of corn, husked and silked

1½ tsp cayenne chili powder

1½ tsp amchur powder or
  chaat masala

1½ tsp kosher salt

1 tsp ground cumin

½ tsp black salt

2 limes, halved

When I think back to vacations in India with my family, I fondly remember visits to Marina Beach in Chennai. Vendors would set up their food stalls on the sand, selling everything from cool drinks to fried fish. Some would grill hearty ears of corn over an open flame until nutty in aroma before smearing them with fiery spices and lime juice. It was the ideal snack as we took in the beauty of the Bay of Bengal and inhaled the salty air of the sea. While roasting over an open flame may not be possible for everyone, this recipe is just as good when the corn is charred on a barbecue or even an indoor grill.

Heat your barbecue or indoor grill to 425°F, or alternatively, place a grill over a gas stove and heat on high. Grill the corn until charred on all sides.

To a small plate, add the chili powder, amchur powder, salt, ground cumin, and black salt. Mix well to combine.

Dip the cut lime into the spice mixture, and rub on the grilled corn, squeezing the lime to release a bit of its juice. Repeat with the remaining ears of corn. Serve warm.

Curry Popcorn Shrimp

SERVES 4

Juice of 1 lemon

2 cloves garlic, finely grated

1 Tbsp ginger, finely grated

½ tsp black pepper

½ tsp cayenne chili powder

½ tsp ground cumin

½ tsp ground coriander

¼ tsp turmeric

¼ tsp granulated sugar

1½ tsp kosher salt

1½ lb (680 g) peeled and deveined shrimp (size 16/20)

1 large egg, whisked

1 cup cornstarch

Canola oil, for deep frying

Lemon wedges, for serving

Coriander Lime Mayo (page 236), for serving

I love the idea of popcorn anything because there's always the perfect ratio of crispy, crunchy coating to ingredient (chicken, shrimp, etc.). This recipe takes this classic snack food and puts an Indian twist on it with a variety of vibrant spices, including smoky black pepper, earthy cumin, and citrusy coriander. Don't say I didn't warn you because you won't be able to stop at just one.

To a large bowl, add the lemon juice, garlic, ginger, pepper, chili powder, ground cumin, ground coriander, turmeric, sugar, and salt and mix until well combined.

Add the shrimp and mix to coat it in the spices. Pour the whisked egg over the shrimp, and mix to combine.

Add the cornstarch to a large resealable plastic bag and drop in a few pieces of shrimp at a time. Seal the bag and shake to coat shrimp with the cornstarch. Remove the shrimp, shaking off any excess cornstarch, and place on a parchment-lined baking sheet. Repeat with the remaining shrimp.

Heat 3 inches (8 cm) of oil in a deep pot or wok to 350°F. Slowly lower in the coated shrimp in batches, ensuring not to crowd the pot. Cook for 4 to 5 minutes until golden and crispy.

Drain on a paper towel. Serve hot with lemon wedges and the mayo.

Paneer Tikka Pizza

For the Paneer Tikka

1½ cups paneer, cut into small dice

2 Tbsp plain yogurt

Juice of ½ lemon

3 cloves garlic, finely grated

½ Tbsp finely grated ginger

1 Tbsp kasoori methi

1 tsp garam masala

2 tsp chaat masala

1 tsp Kashmiri chili powder

1½ tsp kosher salt

For the Sauce

1½ cups strained tomato sauce
   (passata)

1½ tsp garam masala

1 Tbsp kasoori methi

1 tsp cayenne chili powder

1 tsp garlic powder

Kosher salt

For Assembly

1 ball of store-bought pizza dough,
   divided in 2

All-purpose flour, for dusting

3 cups grated mozzarella

½ cup thinly sliced green peppers

½ cup thinly sliced red onions

Fresh coriander (cilantro) leaves,
   for garnish

There always comes a moment on my trips to India when I start craving one of my favorite foods—pizza! While pepperoni might not be on the menu in Indian pizzerias, I have indulged in many local variations that merge Indian and Italian flavors beautifully. The combination of springy marinated paneer flavored with tangy chaat masala and spiced tomato sauce featuring garam masala and kasoori methi makes my version really special. While paneer tikka is typically served with naan, I think featuring it as a topping for pizza is quite fun!

To make the paneer tikka, to a medium bowl, add the paneer, yogurt, lemon juice, garlic, ginger, kasoori methi, garam masala, chaat masala, Kashmiri chili powder, and salt. Toss to combine and let marinate for 15 minutes at room temperature.

To make the sauce, in a small bowl, whisk together the strained tomato sauce, garam masala, kasoori methi, cayenne chili powder, garlic powder, and salt to taste.

Place a pizza stone or cast-iron pizza pan in the oven, and preheat to 500°F.

To assemble, roll out half of the pizza dough on a floured counter (to avoid sticking) until about 10 inches (25 cm) in diameter and about ¼ inch (6 mm) thick. Transfer to a floured pizza peel.

Pour half the sauce in the center of the rolled dough, and gently spread it out, reserving an inch (2.5 cm) of dough for the crust. Top with half the mozzarella, half the green peppers, and half the red onions. Arrange half the marinated paneer evenly overtop. Repeat with the remaining dough, sauce, and toppings (while your first pizza bakes).

Transfer the prepared pizza to the heated pizza stone and bake for 12 to 15 minutes or until the bottom and crust are a deep golden brown and the cheese on top begins to bubble and brown.

Remove from the oven and transfer to a cutting board. Allow to rest for 5 minutes. Garnish with fresh coriander leaves and cut into slices. Enjoy hot!

5-Ingredient Masala Vada

SERVES 6

1 cup chana dhal
  (dried split chickpeas)

1 medium yellow onion,
  finely chopped

4 Thai green chilis, finely minced

¼ cup chopped fresh coriander
  (cilantro)

1 Tbsp finely minced ginger

3 tsp kosher salt

Canola oil, for deep frying

5-Minute Coconut Chutney
  (page 232), for serving

Masala vada is like India's answer to the falafel. A crispy domed fritter made of ground soaked chickpeas flavored with fiery Thai green chilis and ginger, it can be served as part of a full South Indian meal or as a snack at teatime.

Place the chana dhal in a bowl and cover with warm water. Soak for 1½ hours, then drain.

Add the drained chana dhal to a food processor and pulse until the dhal has a coarse texture, and can hold its shape when squeezed in your hands.

Transfer the processed dhal to a large bowl and add the onion, chilis, fresh coriander, ginger, and salt. Mix well to combine.

Heat 3 inches (8 cm) of oil in a deep pot or wok to 350°F.

Take a golf-ball-sized portion of the chana mixture and form into a round patty 2½ inches (6.5 cm) in diameter. The patty should be domed toward the middle and taper off toward the edges. Repeat with the remaining mixture.

Gently place the vadas in the oil in batches, taking care not to crowd the pan, and cook for 4 to 5 minutes, flipping once or twice during frying until deeply golden brown.

Drain onto a paper towel. Serve warm with chutney.

Reshmi Kebabs

SERVES 4

¼ cup whipping (35%) cream

2 Tbsp raw cashews

¼ cup plain yogurt

Juice of ½ lemon

½ Tbsp finely grated ginger

4 cloves garlic, finely grated

2 Thai green chilis, finely minced

¼ cup chopped fresh coriander
  (cilantro)

½ tsp black pepper

¼ tsp nutmeg

1 tsp salt

1½ lb (680 g) chicken breast,
  cut into 2-inch (5 cm) cubes

¼ cup melted ghee

Restaurant-Style Butter Naan
  (page 164), for serving

Mint Coriander Chutney (page 236)

While kebabs can be served as a main course in Indian restaurants, they are often brought out as an appetizer to kick off a meal. It was on a trip to Coimbatore with my parents that I tried a reshmi kebab for the first time and fell in love. The creamy spiced marinade was a unique departure from all the kebabs I had previously tried, and it made a lasting impression on me. (The combination of creamy cashews, green chilis, and nutmeg really sold me!) While these can be served with naan and mint coriander chutney as I have suggested, they are also great all by themselves with a squeeze of lemon.

To make the marinade, begin by blending the cream and cashews in a small blender or food processor until a thick paste forms.

Transfer the cashew paste to a large bowl and add the yogurt, lemon juice, ginger, garlic, chilis, fresh coriander, pepper, nutmeg, and salt. Mix to combine.

Add the chicken breast to the marinade and mix well to coat. Cover and marinate the chicken in the fridge for a minimum of 2 hours to overnight.

Thread the marinated chicken onto soaked bamboo skewers (or metal skewers) and preheat the grill to 400°F. Grill for 5 to 6 minutes on each side, basting periodically with the melted ghee, until slightly charred on the outside and cooked through to the middle.

Serve with naan and chutney.

Boiled Peanut Sundal

SERVES 6

8 cups water

1 Tbsp kosher salt, plus more to taste

3 cups fresh raw peanuts (shell on)

2 Tbsp canola oil

1 tsp black mustard seeds

1 tsp split skinless urad dhal
(black gram)

½ tsp asafoetida

3 Thai green chilis, finely sliced

3 dried red chilis, each broken
into 3 pieces

10 fresh curry leaves (or 2 Tbsp
chopped fresh coriander)

½ cup grated fresh coconut

1 cup peeled and finely diced green
mango (see note on page 227)

Sundal is a dish that reminds me of visiting the temple, and my mom hosting poojas (prayers) at home. It features stir-fried legumes (most often chickpeas), cooked together with coconut and spices until slightly toasty in aroma. My mom adds crunchy raw green mango to her recipe, so I've followed suit—it adds a pop of acidity that complements the nuttiness of the coconut and peanuts really well. This is a great dish to serve as a snack with a cold drink when you're watching your favorite TV show or during cocktail hour.

Bring the water to a boil and season with the salt. Add the peanuts, cover the pot, and boil for 30 minutes. Drain the peanuts, allow to cool slightly, and remove the shells.

Heat the oil on medium-high heat in a large frying pan. Add the black mustard seeds and urad dhal, and cook for 10 seconds or until the urad dhal is slightly golden in color. Add the asafoetida, green chilis, dried red chilis, and curry leaves. Cook for 15 seconds or just until the curry leaves take on a vibrant green color.

Immediately add the shelled peanuts and season with more salt to taste. Sauté for 4 to 5 minutes to warm the peanuts through. Add the coconut and cook for 1 to 2 minutes.

Remove from the heat and stir in the diced green mango.

Vegetables and Legumes

30-Minute Amritsari Chole
Chickpea Curry

SERVES 4

2½ cups water

2 black tea bags (Assam, breakfast, Ceylon, or Darjeeling)

3 Tbsp canola oil

1 bay leaf

1 cinnamon stick

3 green cardamom pods

1 black cardamom pod (optional)

3 cloves

1 medium yellow onion, finely chopped

4 cloves garlic, finely grated

½ Tbsp finely grated ginger

1 cup strained tomato sauce (passata)

1 tsp Kashmiri chili powder

1 tsp garam masala

1 tsp kasoori methi

1 tsp ground coriander

1 tsp amchur powder (optional, see note)

1 tsp anardhana (dried pomegranate) powder (optional, see note)

½ tsp black salt

½ tsp ground turmeric

¼ tsp asafoetida

Kosher salt

2 cans (19 oz/540 ml each) chickpeas, drained and rinsed

2 Tbsp ghee

1 tsp ground cumin

3 long green finger chilis, split lengthwise

Puffy Pooris (page 171), for serving

When I am looking for comfort, I turn to this Amritsari chole. Also known as chana masala, this dish brings together humble chickpeas with an array of spices woven into a rich, deep, and tangy gravy. While this recipe is typically made by soaking and cooking dried chickpeas, I take a handy shortcut by using tinned chickpeas, which cuts back on prep time without compromising flavor or texture. Also, my secret ingredient, black tea, gives this curry its beautiful deep color as well as an herbal back note that makes this curry extra delicious! Be sure to serve this with a pile of thinly sliced red onions and long green chilis on the side for extra crunch and heat, along with my Puffy Pooris (page 171), Kulchas (page 172), 5-Ingredient Chapatis (page 168), or 3-Ingredient Peas Pulao (page 138).

Add the water to a small saucepan and bring it to a boil. Add the tea bags and continue boiling for 3 minutes or until the water takes on a dark brown hue. Remove from the heat and discard the tea bags.

To a large pot on medium heat, add the oil. Once hot, add the bay leaf, cinnamon stick, green cardamom, black cardamom, and cloves. Sauté for 10 to 15 seconds or until the cloves puff up. Add the onion, garlic, and ginger and sauté until softened and fragrant. Pour in the strained tomato sauce and continue cooking for 10 to 15 minutes, stirring frequently, until the tomatoes become jammy and the oil begins to sizzle along the edges of the mixture.

Add the chili powder, garam masala, kasoori methi, ground coriander, amchur powder, anardhana powder, black salt, turmeric, asafoetida, and salt to taste. Mix to combine. Add the drained chickpeas and tea water. Increase the heat to medium-high and simmer for an additional 10 minutes to slightly thicken. Transfer to a serving bowl.

Add the ghee to a small frying pan on medium-high heat. Once hot, sprinkle in the cumin and add the chilis. Cook for 10 seconds and then pour over the prepared chole. Stir to mix in. Serve hot with pooris.

Note: In case amchur and anardhana powders are not available, stir in the juice of ½ large lemon at the end of cooking, before the addition of the spiced ghee.

Vegetable Korma Pot Pie

SERVES 4 TO 6

½ cup raw cashews

1 cup warm water

1½ cups peeled and chopped yellow potatoes

1 cup chopped carrots

1½ cups cauliflower florets

1 cup green beans, cut into 2-inch (5 cm) pieces

1 cup frozen green peas

3 Tbsp ghee

1 bay leaf

1 cinnamon stick

3 green cardamom pods

4 cloves

1 star anise

1 medium yellow onion, finely chopped

4 cloves garlic, finely grated

½ Tbsp finely grated ginger

3 Thai green chilis, finely minced

1 cup canned coconut milk

Salt

1 medium tomato, diced

¼ cup chopped fresh coriander (cilantro)

¼ cup chopped mint

Juice of ½ lemon

1 sheet (8 oz/225 g) frozen puff pastry, thawed

Turning korma into a pot pie filling was a no-brainer for me. This is the perfect way to use up any leftover vegetables you may have hanging out in your crisper drawer. The spiced cashew coconut gravy really makes all the vegetables shine and is wonderful topped with the crispy, buttery puff pastry.

Preheat the oven to 425°F.

Add the cashews and water to a small blender. Blend until a smooth paste forms.

Bring a large pot of water to a boil and add the potatoes and carrots. Boil for 7 to 8 minutes or until they are tender with a bit of bite. Add the cauliflower and green beans and cook for an additional 3 minutes until tender. Lastly, add the peas and immediately drain all vegetables into a colander.

Add the ghee to a large pot on medium heat. Once hot, add the bay leaf, cinnamon stick, green cardamom, cloves, and star anise. Sauté for 15 to 20 seconds, or until the cloves have just puffed up.

Add the onion, garlic, ginger, and chilis and sauté until lightly browned. Add the coconut milk and cashew paste and bring to a simmer. Add the boiled vegetables and stir to coat in the sauce. Season with salt to taste and reduce until thickened.

Remove from the heat and add the tomato, fresh coriander, mint, and lemon juice. Stir to combine.

Pour the korma into a 9 × 13-inch (23 × 33 cm) baking dish, spreading it out into one even layer. Roll out the puff pastry sheet into a 9 × 13-inch (23 × 33 cm) rectangle and place it over the baking dish to cover. Press the pastry along the edges of the dish to create a seal. Cut four ½-inch (1.5 cm) slits along the length of the pastry using a paring knife.

Bake for 25 to 30 minutes or until the pastry is golden and crispy. Allow to rest for 10 minutes before serving.

South Indian Potato Masala

SERVES 6

4 cups peeled yellow potatoes
in medium dice

3 Tbsp ghee

1 tsp split skinless urad dhal
(black gram)

1 tsp black mustard seeds

¼ tsp asafoetida

1 medium yellow onion,
finely chopped

1 Tbsp finely grated ginger

4 Thai green chilis, thinly sliced

½ tsp ground turmeric

Kosher salt

¼ cup chopped fresh coriander
(cilantro)

Puffy Pooris (page 171), for serving

4-Ingredient Dosas (page 175),
for serving

One of the first dishes I ever learned to cook from my mom was this easy potato masala. This is a dish seen regularly on the table in South Indian homes, paired with hot pooris or stuffed into crispy dosas to make masala dosas for breakfast, brunch, or tiffin. However, it's so good that I wouldn't hold back from making it for lunch or dinner either.

Bring a large pot of water to a boil. Add the potatoes and boil until very tender (easily mashable with a fork), about 15 minutes. Reserve 1 cup of the cooking water to use later and drain the potatoes in a colander.

To a large frying pan on medium heat, add the ghee. Add the urad dhal. Once it is golden brown, add the mustard seeds and allow them to sputter and crackle for 10 to 15 seconds. Immediately add the asafoetida, onion, ginger, chilis, and turmeric. Sauté for 2 to 3 minutes, until the onions have softened.

Tip in the cooked potatoes, potato cooking water, and salt to taste. Increase the heat to high and mash the potatoes together with the cooking water. The masala will be a mix of mashed potatoes and potato chunks.

Turn off the heat, sprinkle in the fresh coriander, and stir to combine. Serve with hot pooris or stuff into dosas to make masala dosas.

Express Dhal Makhani

SERVES 4

1 cup whole urad dhal with skin
  (see note)

½ cup dry red kidney beans

4 cups water

1 medium yellow onion,
  finely chopped

4 cloves garlic, finely minced

2-inch (5 cm) knob ginger,
  peeled and finely chopped

1 tsp Kashmiri chili powder

1 tsp ground cumin

1 tsp ground coriander

1 bay leaf

1 cinnamon stick

3 Tbsp ghee

1 tsp cumin seeds

1 cup strained tomato sauce (passata)

Kosher salt

1 Tbsp kasoori methi

4 Thai green chilis, split lengthwise

¼ cup butter

½ cup and 2 Tbsp whipping (35%)
  cream, divided

½ cup chopped fresh coriander
  (cilantro)

2 Tbsp julienned ginger

Classic Basmati Rice (page 137),
  for serving

Restaurant-Style Butter Naan
  (page 164), for serving

Note: The shiny black skin of the urad dhal contributes to the color of this curry and a slightly coarse texture that contrasts with the creamy lentils once they're mashed. This dhal can be found in the international aisle of grocery stores, or at Indian grocery stores and online.

I remember getting my first taste of dhal makhani as a kid and wondering how a vegetarian dish could be so delicious! It's creamy both from the velvety lentils and the cream and butter, slightly smoky from the spices, and tangy from the tomatoes. The key to victory with this recipe is to take the time to mash the dhal and kidney beans until they're somewhat creamy but still retain a bit of texture. While I've suggested a ladle or potato masher to help with this, a quick whiz with an immersion blender will also do the trick! I love eating this curry with my Classic Basmati Rice (page 137) or scooped up with Restaurant-Style Butter Naan (page 164).

Place the urad dhal and kidney beans in a bowl and cover with water. Rinse thoroughly and drain in a colander.

Transfer the rinsed dhal and beans to a multi-cooker or pressure cooker. Add the 4 cups of water, and add the onion, garlic, ginger, chili powder, ground cumin, ground coriander, bay leaf, and cinnamon stick. Pressure cook on high for 30 minutes.

While the dhal and beans are cooking, add the ghee to a frying pan on medium heat. Once hot, add the cumin seeds and let them crackle for 10 to 15 seconds, then add the tomato sauce and season with salt to taste. Cook the tomatoes until they're jammy in texture and the ghee begins to sizzle along the edges of the tomatoes. Season with the kasoori methi and chilis. Stir to combine.

Allow the multi-cooker or pressure cooker to naturally release its pressure, and carefully open the lid. Using the back of a ladle or a potato masher, lightly mash the dhal and beans to create a creamy texture. Then add the cooked tomato mixture and mix to combine.

Place the multi-cooker on sauté mode (or return the pressure cooker to medium heat) and stir in the butter and ½ cup of the cream.

Transfer the dhal to a serving bowl and garnish with a drizzle of the remaining 2 Tbsp of cream and a sprinkle of the fresh coriander and ginger.

Serve hot over rice or with naan for scooping.

15-Minute Spinach Kootu
Spinach Curry with Lentils and Coconut

SERVES 4

1 cup grated fresh coconut
(or frozen grated coconut)

2 tsp cumin seeds

4 Thai green chilis

2½ cups water, divided

1 cup moong dhal (dried split
mung beans)

2 lb (900 g) spinach, chopped

Kosher salt

2 Tbsp ghee

1 tsp split skinless urad dhal
(black gram)

1 tsp black mustard seeds

Classic Basmati Rice (page 137),
for serving

5-Ingredient Chapatis (page 168),
for serving

Every kid was served spinach in some shape or form growing up, and for me, it was this spinach kootu. The hearty combo of the almost melty lentils, wilted spinach, and rich coconut milk in this dish is absolutely sublime. The smell and sound of the hot spiced oil splashing into the spinach at the very end of cooking is a core memory I have held onto since childhood.

To a small blender or coffee grinder, add the coconut, cumin, chilis, and ½ cup of the water. Blend until smooth.

Place the moong dhal in a medium bowl and cover with warm water. Massage the dhal until the water turns cloudy, then drain. Repeat once more.

Add the rinsed dhal and the remaining 2 cups of water to a multi-cooker or pressure cooker. Stir the bottom of the pot to ensure no dhal is sticking. Pressure cook on high for 6 minutes, and then allow the pressure to release naturally.

Remove the lid and bring the dhal back to a simmer. Stir in the spinach. Once the spinach has wilted, pour in the coconut paste and season with salt to taste. Simmer for 1 minute, then remove from the heat.

To a small frying pan on medium-high heat, add the ghee. Once hot, add the urad dhal and toast until lightly golden, 15 to 20 seconds. Add the black mustard seeds and let them crackle for 5 to 10 seconds. Pour the hot spiced ghee into the spinach kootu. Stir to mix.

Serve hot over rice or with chapatis.

Palak Paneer Lasagna

SERVES 6

2 lb (900 g) spinach

12 dry lasagna sheets

2 Tbsp olive oil

1 large tomato, diced

3 Tbsp canola oil

3 Tbsp ghee

1 medium yellow onion,
  finely chopped

6 cloves garlic, finely grated

1½ Tbsp finely grated ginger

1 tsp ground turmeric

1 tsp ground cumin

2 tsp ground coriander

2 tsp Kashmiri chili powder

1½ Tbsp garam masala

1½ cups water

Kosher salt

2 cups whipping (35%) cream

5 cups 1-inch (2.5 cm) cubed paneer

4 cups grated mozzarella cheese

Palak paneer is easily one of my favorite Indian vegetarian dishes of all time. Mellow and creamy, with chunks of springy paneer, it totally made sense to use this curry as a base for lasagna, since it mimics the traditional spinach and ricotta mixture that we see often in classic lasagnas. This is a great dish to introduce Indian flavors to kids and adults alike, because it's not too spicy and uses a favorite pasta to carry the curry.

Preheat the oven to 400°F.

Bring a large pot of water to a rapid boil. Add the spinach, cook for 30 seconds, then remove using a slotted spoon. Set aside.

Season the same pot of boiling water with salt so that it tastes like the sea. Add the lasagna sheets, stirring to keep them from sticking together. Boil for 4 minutes. The noodles will still be very firm. Drain and toss with the olive oil to coat. Lay the noodles flat on a baking sheet.

Add the tomato to a food processor or blender and blend until smooth. Add the cooked spinach and pulse until coarse in texture.

To a medium pot on medium heat, add the oil and ghee. Once hot, add the onion and sauté until softened and golden, 4 to 5 minutes. Add the garlic and ginger, and sauté for 15 to 30 seconds until fragrant.

Sprinkle in the turmeric, cumin, coriander, chili powder, and garam masala. Toast the spices for 10 to 15 seconds. Add the spinach tomato mixture, water, and salt to taste. Bring the mixture to a simmer and cook for 10 to 15 minutes, stirring occasionally, or until the spinach transforms from a bright green to an earthy brown color.

Stir in the cream and simmer for 1 minute. Remove the pan from the heat, add the paneer, and mix to combine.

recipe continues

To assemble the lasagna, cover the base of a 9 × 13-inch (23 × 33 cm) baking dish with ½ cup of the palak paneer. Then layer 4 noodles, one-third of the remaining palak paneer, and one-third of the mozzarella cheese. Repeat the layers twice.

Cover the baking dish with aluminum foil and bake for 45 minutes. Remove the foil and bake for an additional 10 minutes to slightly brown the top.

Let cool for 10 minutes before cutting and serving.

Paneer Butter Masala
Creamy Tomato Curry with Paneer

SERVES 4

2 cups cubed paneer

3 Tbsp canola oil, divided

3 cloves

3 green cardamom pods

1 cinnamon stick

1 bay leaf

2 cups strained tomato sauce (passata)

⅓ cup unsalted butter

1 Tbsp kasoori methi, plus more for garnish

1 Tbsp granulated sugar

1 tsp Kashmiri chili powder

1 tsp garam masala

Kosher salt

1½ cups whipping (35%) cream, plus more for garnish

Restaurant-Style Butter Naan (page 164), for serving

Classic Basmati Rice (page 137), for serving

Several years ago, my family and I visited a temple town in southern India, Rameswaram, and stayed at a hotel that served vegetarian food exclusively (to my and my brother's shock!). While meticulously reviewing the menu, we came across paneer butter masala, and our lives were changed forever. It was the vegetarian equivalent of butter chicken, and that is all we needed to know. A cream-and-tomato-based curry with chunks of springy paneer. Delicious!

Toss the paneer in 1 Tbsp of the oil until well coated. Place in an air fryer and cook at 400°F for 7 to 8 minutes, shaking once or twice until the paneer is golden brown. Or place the paneer in a large nonstick pan on medium-high heat and cook for 5 to 6 minutes, stirring often, until all sides are golden brown. Transfer to a plate.

Add the remaining 2 Tbsp of oil to a large nonstick pan (the same one if you've used a pan in the first step) over medium heat. Add the cloves, cardamom, cinnamon, and bay leaf. Sauté for 10 to 15 seconds, or until the cloves puff up. Add the strained tomato sauce followed by the butter, kasoori methi, sugar, chili powder, garam masala, and salt to taste. Cook the sauce for 15 minutes, stirring frequently, until the tomatoes reduce down and become jammy, and the fats in the pan begin to sizzle along their edges.

Pour in the cream, stir, and bring to a simmer. Fold in the browned paneer, stir it into the curry, and warm for 1 minute.

Plate in a large bowl and garnish with an additional drizzle of cream and a sprinkle of kasoori methi. Serve with naan and/or rice.

Simple Sambar
Spiced Lentil and Vegetable Soup

SERVES 6

1 cup toor dhal (pigeon peas)

6¼ cups water, divided

2 tsp asafoetida, divided

1 tsp ground turmeric

1 medium yellow onion,
 finely chopped

1 large tomato, chopped

2 Thai green chilis, split lengthwise

2 cups chopped Italian eggplant

1 cup 1-inch (2.5 cm) green bean
 pieces

1 large carrot, peeled and sliced
 into ¼-inch (6 mm) rings

½ cup trimmed and halved radishes

¼ cup boiling water

1 Tbsp seedless tamarind pulp
 (see note)

Kosher salt

4 Tbsp ghee

1 tsp black mustard seeds

2 tsp cayenne chili powder

1 tsp ground coriander

10 fresh curry leaves

½ cup chopped fresh coriander
 (cilantro)

Classic Basmati Rice (page 137),
 for serving

4-Ingredient Dosas (page 175),
 for serving

Sambar is a staple dish in South Indian homes. A spiced vegetable and lentil soup, this dish is often served at breakfast as an accompaniment alongside idlis (steamed rice and lentil cakes), dosas (rice and lentil crêpes), pongal (savory lentil and rice porridge), and methu vadas (fried lentil fritters). For lunch and dinner, it is served over hot white rice to make a hearty, filling meal. Every family has their own version, and this is mine.

Place the toor dhal in a bowl and rinse with warm water until the water runs clear. Drain and repeat.

Transfer the drained dhal to a multi-cooker or pressure cooker. Add 6 cups of the water, 1 tsp of the asafoetida, turmeric, and the onion, tomato, chilis, eggplant, green beans, carrot, and radishes. Pressure cook on high for 5 minutes. Allow the multi-cooker or pressure cooker to naturally release its pressure and carefully open the lid.

Pour ¼ cup boiling water over the tamarind and soak for 5 minutes.

Place the multi-cooker in sauté mode (or return the pressure cooker to medium heat). Massage the soaked tamarind with your fingers to gently release the pulp. Strain through a sieve to remove any fibers and pour the tamarind juice and pulp into the cooked dhal and vegetable mixture. Season with salt to taste, and stir to combine.

To a small frying pan on medium heat, add the ghee. Once hot, sprinkle in the mustard seeds and let them crackle for 10 seconds. Remove the pan from the heat and sprinkle in the chili powder, ground coriander, and curry leaves and stir for 5 to 6 seconds. Immediately pour the hot spiced ghee into the dhal. Mix to combine. Lastly, sprinkle with the fresh coriander.

Serve over hot rice or with dosas.

> **Note:** Tamarind can easily be found at Asian grocery stores as well as many large supermarket chains nowadays. It comes in many varieties, including the whole fruit in pods, a concentrated paste that can be found in jars, and blocks with a firm, sticky texture. I prefer using the block variety as it provides a fruity, tangy flavor that elevates Indian dishes without being too overpowering.

Bhindi Masala
Okra Curry

SERVES 4

2 Tbsp canola oil

1 lb (450 g) okra, tops and bottoms trimmed, and halved widthwise

2 Tbsp ghee

1 medium yellow on on, finely chopped

1 tsp cayenne chili powder

½ tsp ground coriander

1 tsp garam masala

½ Tbsp finely grated ginger

2 cloves garlic, finely grated

2 large tomatoes, chopped

Kosher salt

¼ cup chopped fresh coriander (cilantro)

Kulchas (page 172), for serving

5-Ingredient Chapatis (page 168), for serving

Restaurant-Style Butter Naan (page 164), for serving

3-Ingredient Peas Pulao (page 138), for serving

Okra is one of those love/hate vegetables. Often, people find it difficult to get over its sometimes sticky, sappy texture. If you are on the fence, let me convert you with this recipe! A few easy tricks in the cooking process will bring out the okra's prime texture, making you reach for seconds—guaranteed! The okra takes on a beautiful tender texture, with a bit of crunch from the seeds on the inside, and it is coated in a rich, tangy spiced tomato sauce. Easily one of my favorite Indian vegetarian dishes!

Heat the oil in a frying pan on high heat. Add the okra and cook, stirring often, until it has slightly softened and taken on a bright green color, 2 to 3 minutes. Remove the okra from the pan and set aside in a large dish.

Reduce the heat to medium-high and add the ghee to the same frying pan. Add the onion and cook until softened and translucent, 3 to 4 minutes. Add the chili powder, ground coriander, and garam masala. Fry for 10 to 15 seconds to toast the spices. Add the grated ginger and garlic and sauté for another 20 to 30 seconds to soften. Add the tomatoes and season with salt to taste. Cook this mixture for 5 minutes, stirring occasionally until the tomatoes begin to break down.

Return the sautéed okra to the pan and mix into the cooked tomatoes. Cook on medium heat, slightly covered, for 15 minutes, stirring occasionally, until the okra has softened and the tomatoes have become jammy in texture.

Remove from the heat and garnish with fresh coriander. Serve with kulchas, chapatis, naan, and/or peas pulao.

Baingan ka Bharta
Smoky Eggplant Curry

SERVES 4

2 large Italian eggplants, cut lengthwise down the middle

2 Tbsp canola oil

2 Tbsp ghee

1 large yellow onion, finely chopped

½ Tbsp garam masala

1 tsp cayenne chili powder

1 tsp ground coriander

4 cloves garlic, finely chopped

2-inch (5 cm) knob ginger, finely chopped

3 large tomatoes, chopped

Kosher salt

Chopped fresh coriander, for garnish

Kulchas (page 172), for serving

5-Ingredient Chapatis (page 168), for serving

Restaurant-Style Butter Naan (page 164), for serving

My mom is an amazing cook, and her baingan ka bharta is a testament to that! She cleverly roasts and finely chops her eggplant so that it seamlessly blends into the tomato curry base. While she slowly roasts her eggplant whole on the grill or over her gas stove, I've streamlined the process by splitting the eggplant and baking it flesh side down in the oven. Exposing the flesh to the base of the pan allows it to steam quickly in the oven, cutting back on a lot of prep time. Don't hesitate to go with a little more ginger if you like a fresh pop of heat.

Place the eggplants flesh side down on a baking sheet. Place under the broiler and cook until the skin has charred and the flesh has softened, 10 to 12 minutes.

Scoop out the flesh onto a cutting board. Roughly chop and transfer to a bowl.

To a medium pot on medium-high heat, add the oil and ghee. Once hot, add the onion and cook until softened and slightly golden, about 5 to 6 minutes. Sprinkle in the garam masala, chili powder, and coriander. Sauté for 15 seconds or until fragrant. Add the garlic and ginger, and sauté for an additional 15 seconds until softened and fragrant.

Add the tomatoes and cook for 10 to 15 minutes, stirring often, until the mixture is jammy in texture and the fats in the pan begin to sizzle along the edges. Add the roasted eggplant and season with salt to taste. Cook for an additional 5 minutes to warm the eggplant through.

Garnish with fresh coriander and serve with kulchas, chapatis, or naan.

Poultry
and Eggs

5-Ingredient Masala Omelet

3 large eggs

Kosher salt

2½ Tbsp ghee, divided

⅓ cup finely diced red onions

2 Thai green chilis, finely minced

1 small tomato, seeded and diced

2 slices white bread

Waking up in the morning as a kid, I knew when my mom was making a masala omelet because the fragrance of the sweet onions and fiery chilis frying up in the pan was so distinctive and alluring. She would go the extra mile by smearing ghee on white bread and toasting it in the pan until buttery and crisp to serve alongside the omelet. While I picked out the chilis as a kid, I can fully appreciate the little pops of heat with every bite as an adult.

Crack the eggs into a bowl and season with salt to taste. Whisk until well combined.

Heat a frying pan on medium heat. Add 1½ Tbsp of the ghee. Once hot, add the onions and chilis, and sauté for 15 to 20 seconds or until slightly softened and fragrant. Add the tomato and give the mixture a quick stir just to warm through.

Using a spatula, spread out the vegetables in the pan so that they are evenly distributed. Pour in the whisked eggs and swirl the pan so that the eggs cover the bottom. Cook for 1½ minutes or until golden brown on the bottom. Flip and cook for an additional 30 to 45 seconds to set the other side, then transfer to a plate.

Spread the remaining 1 Tbsp of ghee onto both sides of each slice of bread. Place in the same frying pan, and cook on medium-high heat, flipping once, until golden brown on both sides.

Serve the omelet with the toasted bread alongside.

The Best Butter Chicken

SERVES 4

For the Chicken

½ cup plain yogurt

Juice of 1 lemon

2 tsp garam masala

1 tsp Kashmiri chili powder

1 tsp ground coriander

1 tsp ground turmeric

Kosher salt

1½ lb (680 g) boneless skinless chicken thighs, cut into bite-sized pieces

3 Tbsp ghee

For the Sauce

½ cup unsalted butter

2 cups strained tomato sauce (passata)

1 Tbsp sugar

1 tsp Kashmiri chili powder

1½ tsp garam masala

2 Tbsp kasoori methi, divided

Kosher salt

2 cups whipping (35%) cream, plus more for garnish

3-Ingredient Peas Fulao (page 138), for serving

Restaurant-Style Butter Naan (page 164), for serving

I am not one to toot my own horn, but this recipe is one of my best of all time, garnering millions of views on YouTube. It does not require onions, garlic, or ginger (which often surprises people), but delivers on flavor big time! Creamy and rich, with the perfect balance between tomato, cream, and spices, this recipe is one you'll come back to time and time again. The ultimate accompaniments for this dish? Peas pulao and naan. You can't go wrong!

To make the chicken, add the yogurt, lemon juice, garam masala, chili powder, ground coriander, and turmeric to a bowl. Season with salt to taste and mix until well combined. Add the cut chicken thighs to the yogurt mixture and stir to coat. Cover and marinate for 10 minutes at room temperature.

Heat a large pot or Dutch oven on medium-high heat. Once hot, add the ghee and arrange the marinated chicken evenly in the pot, ensuring not to crowd the pot and working in batches if necessary. Brown the chicken for 2 to 3 minutes on each side, then transfer to a bowl. The chicken does not need to be cooked all the way through at this point.

To make the sauce, reduce the heat to medium and add the butter, strained tomato sauce, sugar, chili powder, garam masala, and 1 Tbsp of the kasoori methi to the pot, and season with salt to taste. Cook on medium to medium-low heat, stirring often, for 15 minutes or until the tomatoes have reduced to a jammy consistency and the fats in the pot begin to sizzle along the edges.

Pour in the cream and mix until a creamy blush-colored sauce forms. Bring to a simmer and add the chicken. Simmer, stirring occasionally, until the chicken has completely cooked through, about 10 minutes.

Transfer to a serving dish and garnish with a drizzle of cream and a sprinkling of the remaining 1 Tbsp kasoori methi.

Serve with peas pulao and naan.

Hariyali Spatchcock Roast Chicken

SERVES 4

1½ cups fresh spinach

1 cup fresh coriander (cilantro)

1 cup fresh mint leaves

4 Thai green chilis

4 cloves garlic

2-inch (5 cm) knob ginger, sliced

Juice of 2 lemons

1 Tbsp garam masala

¾ tsp ground cloves

½ tsp black pepper

2 Tbsp canola oil

2 tsp kosher salt

½ cup plain yogurt

1 whole chicken (5 lb/2.3 kg)

1 cup thinly sliced sweet onions,
  for serving

4 wedges of lemon, for serving

Restaurant-Style Butter Naan
  (page 164), for serving

Mint Coriander Chutney (page 236),
  for serving

I fondly remember my first time tasting hariyali kebab in India. I was floored by its amazing Incredible Hulk–like green color and fresh and zesty flavor. This marinade is incredibly versatile, and I knew it would be the perfect way to give a classic roast chicken a nice pop of flavor. Spatchcocking—removing the backbone of the chicken and laying it flat—helps speed the roasting process of the chicken and makes sure that every part is browned beautifully. Definitely worth the tiny bit of extra effort!

Preheat the oven to 425°F and line a baking sheet with parchment paper.

To a blender, add the spinach, fresh coriander, mint, chilis, garlic, ginger, lemon juice, garam masala, cloves, pepper, oil, and salt. Blend until smooth.

Place the yogurt in a large bowl and add the blended spinach mixture. Stir until well combined.

To prepare the chicken, flip it over so that the spine is facing up. Using a pair of sharp kitchen shears or a knife, cut along each side of the spine and remove the spine. Push down on both sides of the chicken to start flattening it out. Then turn the chicken over so that it is breast side up. Turn the thighs so that they are facing outward and push down on the breasts so that they completely flatten.

Place the flattened chicken in the marinade and mix until completely covered and coated. If you are looking to cook the chicken immediately, you can speed up the marination process by massaging the chicken for 10 minutes to push the flavor of the marinade into the meat before going to the next step. Otherwise, cover and refrigerate for 2 hours.

Place the marinated chicken, breast side up, on the prepared baking sheet. Bake for 1 hour, or until the internal temperature of the thickest part of the chicken (thigh) reads 165°F. Cut into the thickest part of the thigh, and if the juices run clear, you are good to go!

Let rest for 10 minutes before carving. Serve with sliced sweet onions with a sprinkle of salt, wedges of lemon, naan, and chutney.

Achari Chicken Curry

SERVES 4

3 Tbsp canola oil

1 tsp cumin seeds

1 tsp black mustard seeds

1 tsp fennel seeds

1 tsp nigella seeds (kalonji seeds)

4 Thai green chilis, split lengthwise

1 medium red onion, finely chopped

2 Tbsp grated ginger

1 Tbsp grated garlic

2 tsp Kashmiri chili powder

1 tsp ground turmeric

1½ cups strained tomato sauce (passata)

Kosher salt

2 Tbsp chopped Indian pickle (like mango, lime, or garlic)

2 tsp white vinegar

4 chicken drumsticks (1 lb/450 g)

4 chicken thighs (1 lb/450 g), cut in half with a cleaver (bone-in, skin-off)

1 cup plain yogurt, whisked until smooth

Classic Basmati Rice (page 137), for serving

5-Ingredient Chapatis (page 168), for serving

Many Indian meals are accompanied by tart and spicy pickles on the side to provide some contrast and brightness. This addictive flavor profile is woven into this chicken curry through the use of popular North Indian pickling spices and the addition of chopped store-bought pickles. The result is a curry that is not only fragrant, but also distinctly tangy and rich.

To a large pot on medium heat, add the oil. Once hot, add the cumin seeds, black mustard seeds, fennel seeds, and nigella seeds. Toast for 10 to 15 seconds or until the black mustard just finishes popping.

Add the chilis and onion, and sauté for 4 to 5 minutes or until softened and translucent. Add the grated ginger and garlic and cook for 30 to 45 seconds, until fragrant. Add the chili powder and turmeric and stir for a minute to toast the spices.

Pour in the tomato sauce and season with salt to taste. Cook for 15 minutes, stirring occasionally, until the tomatoes have reduced down to a jammy consistency and the fats in the pan begin to sizzle along the edges of the tomato mixture.

Stir in the pickle and vinegar. Add the chicken pieces and mix well to coat in the sauce. Reduce the heat to medium-low, cover the pan, and cook for 15 minutes or until the chicken has completely cooked through. The chicken will be opaque throughout and will have taken on a reddish-orange tinge from the sauce.

Reduce the heat to low and slowly stir in the yogurt until it blends into the sauce. Increase the heat to medium and simmer for an additional 10 minutes.

Serve with hot rice and chapatis on the side for scooping.

15-Minute Egg Bhurji

SERVES 2

4 Tbsp ghee, divided

1 tsp cumin seeds

1 medium red onion, finely chopped

2 Thai green chilis, finely minced

1 Tbsp peeled and finely minced ginger

1 tsp ground turmeric

1 tsp Kashmiri chili powder

1 tsp garam masala

1 tsp amchur powder

½ tsp ground fennel seed

1 medium tomato, finely chopped

Kosher salt

6 large eggs, whisked

¼ cup chopped fresh coriander (cilantro)

4 slices white bread

5-ingredient Chapatis (page 168), for serving

I am a big fan of classic scrambled eggs; however, when I am looking for a little spice to wake up my taste buds, I reach for this recipe. Bhurji features eggs that are scrambled together with onions, chilis, spices, and tomatoes until creamy curds form. Although eggs are often classified as a breakfast food, this dish can be served at any time of the day. For breakfast, I like eating bhurji alongside ghee-griddled toast, while for lunch or dinner, I love scooping it up with chapatis.

To a large frying pan on medium heat, add 2 Tbsp of the ghee. Once hot, add the cumin seeds and toast for 10 to 15 seconds. Add the onion, chilis, and ginger, and sauté for 2 to 3 minutes, or until softened and fragrant.

Sprinkle in the turmeric, chili powder, garam masala, amchur, and fennel. Toast the spices for 15 to 20 seconds, until fragrant.

Add the tomato and season with salt to taste. Cook the tomato for 5 to 7 minutes, or until slightly reduced down to a saucy texture.

Reduce the heat to low and add the whisked eggs. Mix the eggs into the tomato mixture until they are well combined. Increase the heat to medium and continue to stir until the eggs begin to form soft curds. Continue cooking the eggs if you prefer a firmer end result (see note). Remove from the heat and stir in the fresh coriander.

Spread the remaining 2 Tbsp of ghee onto both sides of each slice of bread. Place in a frying pan on medium-high heat, flipping once, until golden brown on both sides.

Serve the bhurji with the ghee-griddled toast as a part of your favorite breakfast spread or chapatis for lunch or dinner.

Note: While I personally like a soft scramble, don't hesitate to cook the eggs a little longer if you like them more firm.

Tandoori Fried Chicken Wings with Spicy Lime Honey

SERVES 4

For the Chicken

2 lb (900 g) chicken wings (drumettes and flats)

½ cup buttermilk

Juice of 1 lime

4 cloves garlic, finely grated

2-inch (5 cm) knob ginger, finely grated

2 Tbsp garam masala, divided

½ tsp powdered or gel red food coloring (optional)

2 Tbsp kosher salt, plus more to taste, divided

2 cups all-purpose flour

½ Tbsp ground ginger

½ Tbsp Kashmiri chili powder

½ Tbsp kasoori methi

½ tsp ground nutmeg

Canola oil, for deep frying

For the Spicy Lime Honey

½ cup honey

Juice and zest of 1 lime

1 Tbsp sriracha

Kosher salt

Lime wedges, for serving

Tandoori is such a revered, classic preparation that you almost want to leave it as is forever. That is, until you realize deep-fried tandoori wings are totally delicious! While they may not be prepared in a classic tandoor oven, these crispy wings take on the flavor of the tandoori marinade beautifully, and are further complemented by the spicy lime honey, which adds a pop of tang, heat, and sweetness. These are perfect on their own or paired with a pile of hot French fries sprinkled with chili powder and salt.

To make the chicken, place the chicken wings in a large bowl. Add the buttermilk, lime juice, garlic, ginger, 1 Tbsp of the garam masala, red food coloring, and salt to taste. Mix well, cover, and marinate for 2 hours in the fridge.

To a large resealable plastic bag, add the flour, ground ginger, chili powder, kasoori methi, nutmeg, and 2 Tbsp of salt. Seal and shake the bag to mix the ingredients.

Add a few chicken wings to the bag at a time, seal, and shake to coat in the flour. Shake any excess flour off of each wing, and transfer to a baking sheet. Repeat this process for all the wings.

Add 3 inches (8 cm) of oil to a wok or large pot on medium-high heat. Once the temperature of the oil is around 375°F, gently lower in a few wings at a time, being careful not to crowd the pan. Cook the wings for 7 to 8 minutes or until they're well browned and crispy. Drain on a wire rack placed over a baking sheet.

To make the spicy lime honey, add the honey, lime juice and zest, sriracha, and salt to a bowl and whisk together.

Serve the wings with the spicy lime honey and extra wedges of lime on the side.

South Indian Egg Masala

SERVES 2

6 large eggs

2 Tbsp canola oil

1 medium yellow onion, finely chopped

1 tsp Kashmiri chili powder

½ tsp ground turmeric

½ tsp ground coriander

½ tsp ground fennel seed

2 cloves garlic, finely grated

1-inch (2.5 cm) knob ginger, peeled and finely grated

1 medium tomato, finely chopped

Kosher salt

¼ cup water

2 to 3 Tbsp chopped fresh coriander (cilantro)

5-Ingredient Chapatis (page 168), for serving

Classic Basmati Rice (page 137), for serving

This is one of my mom's egg-cellent recipes (sorry, I had to!) that she has made ever since we were little kids. I still remember how the tomato gravy would cling to the eggs, and the beautiful yellow hue the eggs took on the longer they sat. While I used to scrape off the sauce as a kid, I would never dare do that now! The combo of the tangy spiced sauce and the delicate yolk is just sensational! These eggs are delicious eaten with chapatis or hot basmati rice.

Arrange the eggs in 1 layer in a small saucepan and cover with water. Bring the water to a boil. Once at a boil, turn off the heat and cover the pan with a lid. Let the eggs sit for 10 minutes. Drain and rinse with cool water. Peel the eggs, discarding the shells, and set aside.

To a medium nonstick frying pan on medium-high heat, add the oil. Once hot, add the onion and sauté for 3 to 4 minutes or until softened and translucent. Add the chili powder, turmeric, ground coriander, and ground fennel. Toast the spices for 15 to 20 seconds. Add the garlic and ginger and cook for 30 seconds or until fragrant.

Add the chopped tomato, and season with salt to taste. Cook the tomato for 4 to 5 minutes or until it starts to break down. Reduce the temperature to low and cover with a lid. Cook the tomato for 3 to 4 minutes or until jammy in consistency.

Remove the lid and increase the heat to medium-high, cooking the tomato until it reduces into a paste and the fats in the pan begin to collect around the edges of the paste. Stir in the water to create a thick sauce.

Gently lower the eggs into the pan, and coat with the masala. Continue cooking for 2 to 3 minutes, turning the eggs often, until the sauce reduces down and the eggs take on a golden hue.

Garnish with fresh coriander. Serve with chapatis or hot basmati rice.

Chicken Pepper Fry

SERVES 4

2 lb (900 g) boneless skinless chicken thighs cut into small pieces

2 tsp turmeric

6 cloves garlic, finely grated, divided

2-inch (5 cm) knob ginger, finely grated, divided

2 tsp kosher salt, plus more to taste

¼ cup canola oil

2 cups finely chopped red onion

5 Thai green chilis, minced (see note)

15 fresh curry leaves

1 Tbsp black peppercorns, coarsely ground in a mortar and pestle

Juice of 1½ lemons

¼ cup chopped fresh coriander (cilantro)

5-Ingredient Chapatis (page 168), for serving

Classic Basmati Rice (page 137), for serving

Plain yogurt, for serving

This dish is a staple in Tamil Nadu and highlights the smoky fragrance and heat of black peppercorns. On our trips to India growing up, we would often order this dish as takeout to eat at home. It would come wrapped in a fresh banana leaf, which would add a beautiful aroma to the chicken and make the entire experience of eating the dish so much more special. Spicy, tangy, and fragrant, this dish is a showstopper of flavors!

To a large bowl, add the chicken, turmeric, half the garlic, half the ginger, and 2 tsp salt. Mix until the chicken is well coated and marinate for 10 minutes at room temperature.

Add the oil to a large frying pan or wok over medium heat. Once hot, add the onions and sauté until golden brown. Add the remaining garlic and ginger, and sauté for 1 minute or until fragrant. Add the chilis and curry leaves, and cook for 15 to 30 seconds.

Increase the heat to high and add the chicken. Mix to coat with the ingredients in the pan, and season with additional salt to taste. Reduce the heat to medium-low, cover, and cook for 15 minutes or until the chicken is cooked through.

Remove the lid and season the chicken with the pepper. Mix and allow the majority of excess moisture in the pan to evaporate, about 10 minutes, stirring occasionally. Add the lemon juice and cook for 1 minute more.

Remove from the heat and garnish with the fresh coriander. Serve with chapatis or basmati rice with a big dollop of yogurt on the side.

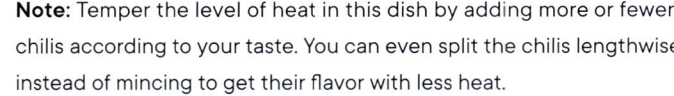

Note: Temper the level of heat in this dish by adding more or fewer chilis according to your taste. You can even split the chilis lengthwise instead of mincing to get their flavor with less heat.

Chicken Cafreal

SERVES 4

6 chicken legs (thigh and
   drumstick attached)

3 cups chopped fresh coriander
   (cilantro)

3-inch (8 cm) knob ginger, sliced

6 cloves garlic

3 Thai green chilis

5 cloves

1 Tbsp coriander seeds

2 tsp black peppercorns

3 tsp cumin seeds

2-inch (5 cm) cinnamon stick

Juice of 1 lemon

Kosher salt

¼ cup canola oil

1 cup water

Potato wedges or French fries,
   for serving

Lemon wedges, for serving

Hailing from the state of Goa, chicken cafreal is a fragrant and tangy green curry flavored with lots of fresh coriander and spices. The recipe is very simple, as the majority of the work is done in a blender. Just blend, marinate, and fry! While I wouldn't hesitate to eat this dish with a heap of hot rice, it is traditionally served with potato wedges or fries and additional wedges of lemon on the side. For a refreshing side, consider serving this with my colorful Kachumber Salad (page 228).

Cut 2 to 3 shallow slits on each piece of the chicken, about ⅜ inch (1 cm) deep, and set aside.

To a blender, add the fresh coriander, ginger, garlic, chilis, cloves, coriander seeds, peppercorns, cumin, cinnamon, lemon juice, and salt to taste. Blend until smooth.

Pour the marinade over the chicken and mix to coat. Cover and marinate in the fridge for 3 to 4 hours. If you are pressed for time, massage the marinade into the chicken for 10 minutes before proceeding to the next step.

Add the oil to a large wok or Dutch oven on medium-high heat. Once hot, add a few pieces of chicken to the pan at a time, being careful not to overcrowd the pan. Brown for 3 to 4 minutes on each side, and transfer to a bowl. At this point, the chicken doesn't have to be cooked through.

Add any remaining marinade to the pan and cook for 3 to 4 minutes or until slightly thickened. Add the water and bring to a simmer. Return all the chicken pieces to the pan and baste with the sauce. It is okay for the chicken pieces to touch each other at this point.

Simmer for 20 to 25 minutes, until the gravy reduces to coat the chicken in a thick sauce.

Serve with potato wedges or French fries and wedges of lemon.

Classic Chicken Tikka Masala

SERVES 4

For the Chicken

½ cup plain yogurt

Juice of ½ lemon

4 cloves garlic, finely grated

1 Tbsp finely grated ginger

2 tsp garam masala

1 tsp kosher salt

1½ lb (680 g) boneless skinless chicken thighs, cut into 1-inch (2.5 cm) pieces

2 Tbsp canola oil

For the Sauce

2 Tbsp unsalted butter

1 large yellow onion, finely diced

4 cloves garlic, finely grated

1-inch (2.5 cm) knob ginger, finely grated

½ tsp ground turmeric

1 tsp ground coriander

1 tsp ground cumin

1 tsp garam masala

2 cups strained tomato sauce (passata)

1 tsp Kashmiri chili powder

Kosher salt

1 cup whipping (35%) cream

¼ cup chopped fresh coriander (cilantro)

Classic Basmati Rice (page 137), for serving

Restaurant-Style Butter Naan (page 164), for serving

With over four million views on YouTube, it is safe to say that chicken tikka masala is my most popular recipe of all time. With roots in Scotland, and having been popularized in the UK and all over the world, this rich and creamy dish hits all the marks of a delicious curry. I like featuring this tikka masala as part of a dinner party spread, as it is mellow and not too spicy, making it a crowd pleaser.

To prepare the chicken, place the yogurt, lemon juice, garlic, ginger, garam masala, and salt into a large bowl. Whisk to combine. Add the chicken and mix to coat in the marinade. Marinate for 10 minutes at room temperature.

To a large pot or Dutch oven on medium heat, add the oil. Once hot, add the chicken pieces, making sure not to crowd the pan (this may be done in batches). Cook for 2 to 3 minutes a side, until browned. The chicken does not have to be cooked through at this stage. Transfer to a bowl.

To make the sauce, to the same pot, add the butter and onion and cook until softened and translucent, 4 to 5 minutes. Add the garlic and ginger and sauté for 30 to 45 seconds or until fragrant. Sprinkle in the turmeric, ground coriander, ground cumin, and garam masala. Sauté for 15 seconds to toast the spices.

Add the tomato sauce and chili powder, and season with salt to taste. Simmer for 15 to 20 minutes on low heat, stirring occasionally, until the tomatoes reduce down to a jammy consistency and the fats in the pan begin to collect along their edges.

Add the browned chicken and pour in the cream. Stir and simmer for an additional 10 minutes, or until the mixture is bubbling, glossy, and thick.

Garnish with the fresh coriander. Serve with hot rice or naan.

Seafood

Hakka-Style Shrimp Pakora

SERVES 4 TO 6

2 lb (900 g) peeled and deveined shrimp (size 16/20), cut into big chunks

2 tsp grated garlic

2 tsp grated ginger

4 Thai green chilis, finely minced

½ tsp garam masala

½ tsp ground cumin

1 tsp kosher salt

1 Tbsp soy sauce

Juice of ½ lemon

1 cup chickpea flour

½ cup cornstarch

½ tsp baking powder

⅓ cup chopped fresh coriander (cilantro)

¼ cup water

Canola oil, for frying

Lemon wedges, for serving

I had my very first taste of Hakka Chinese food when I was a teenager and fell head-over-heels in love with the combination of flavors blended between Indian and Chinese cuisine. The dishes often featured the trinity of garlic, ginger, and Thai green chilis, which brought an irresistible heat and fragrance. These pakoras are crunchy on the outside and super tender and juicy in the middle. They are great paired with Manchurian Shrimp (page 108) and Classic Basmati Rice (page 137) to make a complete meal.

To a large bowl, add the shrimp, garlic, ginger, chilis, garam masala, cumin, salt, soy sauce, and lemon juice. Mix well to combine and marinate for 10 minutes at room temperature.

Add the chickpea flour, cornstarch, baking powder, fresh coriander, and water. Mix again, until the shrimp are nicely coated and no traces of flour can be seen.

Heat 3 inches (8 cm) of oil in a large, deep pot or wok on medium-high heat to 375°F. Gently lower large spoonfuls of the shrimp mixture into the oil to form small fritters. Work in small batches so as not to crowd the pot. Fry for 4 to 5 minutes or until golden and crispy on the outside and cooked through to the middle. A telltale sign that the pakoras are done is when the bubbles around the pakoras begin to die down. Drain onto a large plate lined with paper towel.

Serve hot with lemon wedges on the side.

Fish Kebab Po'boys

SERVES 4

For the Kebabs

1½ lb (680 g) king fish or
  grouper steaks

1 small red onion, finely chopped

2 Tbsp finely chopped ginger

2 Tbsp finely chopped garlic

4 Thai green chilis, thinly sliced

⅓ cup chopped fresh coriander
  (cilantro)

Juice of ½ lemon

Kosher salt

2 large eggs

Canola oil, for frying

For Assembly

2 baguettes

4 Tbsp butter

½ cup mayonnaise

1 cup finely shredded
  iceberg lettuce

½ cup thinly sliced red onion

Lemon wedges

My mom's recipe for fish kebabs is just excellent. They are crispy on the outside and flavored so well with the simple combination of red onions, ginger, garlic, and chilis. Most of my fish consumption as a kid can be credited to these kebabs! While they are delicious on their own with just a squeeze of lemon, I couldn't help but stuff them in a bun to make an epic sandwich. The result is a portable feast with explosive flavor that can be served hot or at room temperature. Take them to the beach or on a picnic, or just hang out in your backyard and feast away.

Place the fish steaks in a steamer basket. Steam for 10 minutes or until completely cooked through. Allow to cool until easy to handle.

Flake the fish into a bowl, discarding any bones and skin. Add the red onion, ginger, garlic, chilis, fresh coriander, lemon juice, and salt to taste. Mix well to combine.

Add the eggs and mix well to combine. Shape the kebabs into 3-inch-long (8 cm) quenelle shapes (pointy on the ends and round in the middle).

Heat 2 inches (5 cm) of oil in a large nonstick frying pan on medium-high heat. Once the oil reaches a temperature of 350°F, gently lower in the kebabs, cooking in batches if necessary to avoid crowding the pan. Cook for 5 to 6 minutes, turning the kebabs 2 to 3 times, until crispy and golden all over. Drain on a paper towel–lined plate.

To assemble the po'boys, slice the baguettes in half widthwise. Take 1 half and cut it lengthwise to create a pocket without completely cutting through. Spread 1 Tbsp of butter along the inside of the baguette. Then place the baguette cut side down on a frying pan and toast for 2 minutes on both sides until warm and golden.

Spread the mayonnaise on the bottom of the baguette and top with a generous handful of lettuce. Arrange the kebabs on top of the lettuce and layer the sliced red onion on top. Fold the top of the baguette over and serve with lemon wedges on the side.

4-Ingredient Tamil Nadu Fish Fry

SERVES 4 TO 6

4 whole red snappers (or 4 grouper
   steaks or 4 skin-on salmon fillets)
   (about 4 lb/2 kg)

3 Tbsp ground coriander

1 Tbsp cayenne chili powder

Juice of 2 limes

Kosher salt

Canola oil, for frying

Wedges of lemon, for serving

Sliced red onion, for serving

Classic Basmati Rice (page 137),
   for serving

Tamil Nadu is a state in South India where my family is from. With a huge coastline, Tamil Nadu has a cuisine that features lots of seafood, with one of the most iconic dishes being fish fry. A staple in many households, and served by vendors beachside, this dish highlights any variety of fish with a simple fiery marinade. Make things simple by getting your local fishmonger to clean the whole fish for you, or swap for fish steaks or fillets if you don't want to deal with all the bones. While this is a great standalone dish served with wedges of lemon and crunchy sweet onion, you can also serve it with a pile of hot basmati rice.

With a sharp knife, create 2 to 3 slits along the length of each snapper. Repeat on the other side, and place on a large plate. If using fillets or steaks, leave the fish as is.

To a small bowl, add the ground coriander, chili powder, lime juice, and salt to taste. Mix to form a paste.

Smear the spice paste all over the red snapper (inside and outside) and marinate in the fridge for 15 minutes.

Heat ½ inch (1.5 cm) of oil in a large nonstick frying pan on medium-high heat. Once the oil reaches a temperature of 350°F, gently lower the snapper into the pan, cooking in batches if necessary to avoid overcrowding the pan. Cook for 4 to 5 minutes on each side or until crispy and golden. Drain on a paper towel–lined plate.

Serve with lemon wedges, sliced onion, and basmati rice on the side.

Salmon Puttu

SERVES 4

3 salmon steaks (about 1½ lb/700 g)

1 Tbsp canola oil

1 small red onion, finely chopped

1 tsp Kashmiri chili powder

1 tsp ground fennel seed

½ tsp ground turmeric

2 Tbsp chopped garlic

2 Tbsp finely chopped ginger

Kosher salt

Juice of ½ lime

½ cup chopped fresh coriander (cilantro)

Puttu is a dish of finely flaked fish sautéed with spices and aromatics. The fennel in this recipe is particularly delicious as it brings an anise-like note to the fish, which helps cut the richness. Traditionally, this dish is made with shark, but I thought salmon would make a great swap because it's easy to find. This is an excellent recipe to share with those tiptoeing into seafood, because of its fine texture and bright flavors. I like serving it with chapatis, but it also makes a great stuffing for a melt or grilled cheese.

Place the salmon steaks in 1 even layer in a steamer. Steam for 10 minutes, or until completely cooked through. Allow to cool until easy to handle.

Flake the salmon into a bowl, discarding any skin and bones. Set aside.

To a large frying pan on medium-high heat, add the oil. Once hot, add the red onion and sauté for 3 to 4 minutes or until softened and translucent. Add the chili powder, fennel seed, and turmeric, mixing the spices into the onion. Toast the spices for 15 to 20 seconds.

Add the garlic and ginger and cook for 15 to 30 seconds until fragrant. Add the flaked salmon, and season with salt to taste. Increase the heat to high, and stir to coat the salmon with the onion mixture. Cook for 3 to 4 minutes or until the salmon is warmed through.

Remove from the heat, squeeze in the lime juice, and garnish with the fresh coriander. Mix well and enjoy!

20-Minute Coconut Fish Korma

SERVES 4

1 Tbsp canola oil

1 Tbsp ghee

3 green cardamom pods

2 cloves

1 star anise

1 cinnamon stick

1 bay leaf

1 medium yellow onion, finely chopped

4 Thai green chilis

5 cloves garlic

2-inch (5 cm) knob ginger, peeled and sliced

¼ cup raw cashews

2 cups water, divided

2 cups canned coconut milk

Kosher salt

4 grouper steaks (about 2 lb/1 kg)

1 medium tomato, quartered

¼ cup chopped fresh coriander (cilantro)

¼ cup chopped mint

Juice of ½ lemon

Classic Basmati Rice (page 137), for serving

When I think of this korma, I imagine myself wrapped in a big warm blanket, because it is pure comfort! The combination of the warm spices and the kick of the Thai green chili simmered in the thickened creamy coconut broth is magic, and really highlights the flavor of any fish you simmer in it. While you can use boneless chunks of a firm-fleshed white fish in this recipe, I do recommend steaks, as the bones contribute to the depth of flavor of the broth. The best part about this recipe is that it takes no time to put together, as most of the heavy lifting is done by the canned coconut milk. Moreover, since the broth is on the lighter side, it picks up the flavor of the aromatics (onions, chilis, garlic, and ginger) very quickly.

To a large pot on medium heat, add the oil and ghee. Once the oil is hot, add the cardamom, cloves, star anise, cinnamon stick, and bay leaf. Sauté for 15 to 20 seconds, until fragrant. Add the onion, and sauté for 3 to 4 minutes or until softened and translucent.

To a small blender, add the chilis, garlic, and ginger, and blend into a smooth paste. Add this paste to the onions and cook for 15 to 20 seconds, until fragrant.

To the same blender, add the cashews and ½ cup of the water. Blend until a smooth cream forms.

Add the remaining 1½ cups of water to the pot, followed by the cashew cream, coconut milk, and salt to taste. Increase the heat to medium-high and bring to a simmer.

Reduce the heat to medium and gently lower in the grouper steaks. Spoon some of the coconut broth over the steaks, cover the pot, and let the fish gently cook for 8 minutes or until almost cooked through. Add the quartered tomato, cover the pot again, and simmer for an additional 2 minutes or until the fish has completely cooked through.

Remove from the heat and gently stir in the fresh coriander, mint, and lemon juice. Serve with hot rice.

Mom's 30-Minute Green Masala Crab

SERVES 4

1 large red onion, coarsely chopped

5 cloves garlic

2-inch (5 cm) knob ginger, sliced

1 large tomato, cut into big chunks

2 cups chopped fresh coriander (cilantro)

2 Thai green chilis

1 tsp black peppercorns

Juice of 1 lemon

Kosher salt

2 Tbsp canola oil

2 cups water

3 lb (1.4 kg) Dungeness crab, cut into large pieces (or blue crabs) (see note)

Classic Basmati Rice (page 137), for serving

This was the fun and messy meal that we loved growing up. My mom would lay newspaper on the table to capture any flying green masala and/or crab shells, and then it was a free-for-all. Our fingers would be covered in masala as we cracked open the crabs to reveal their flesh. The contrast between the herby, spicy sauce and the sweet, tender crab was just divine! This is a super-easy recipe, as the sauce is made in a blender. Ask your local fishmonger to cut the crab for you, and then it's just a matter of adding it to the sauce and letting it simmer, and you're good to go!

Add the onion, garlic, ginger, tomato, fresh coriander, chilis, peppercorns, lemon juice, and salt to taste to a blender. Blend until smooth.

Heat the oil in a large wok or pot on medium heat. Once hot, add the green masala and cook for 3 to 4 minutes or until slightly reduced. Add the water, stir, and increase the heat to high. Cook the sauce until it's bubbling and slightly thickened, about 5 minutes.

Add the crab pieces and mix to coat in the sauce. Cover the pan with a lid and cook the crab for 10 to 12 minutes or until the shells take on a reddish-orange hue and the flesh on the inside is opaque.

Serve with rice.

Note: Crab can most often be found at Asian supermarkets. Don't hesitate to ask the fishmonger to cut the crab for you, as they are often more than willing. Otherwise, cut the crab with a heavy cleaver.

Crispy Green Chili Calamari with Lemon Cumin Aioli

SERVES 2

For the Calamari

1 lb (450 g) calamari, cleaned and cut into ¾-inch (2 cm) rings

Juice of ½ lemon

2 cloves garlic, finely grated

1-inch (2.5 cm) knob ginger, finely grated

3 Thai green chilis, finely minced

Kosher salt

1½ cups all-purpose flour

½ cup cornstarch

½ tsp baking powder

½ tsp black pepper

Canola oil, for frying

For the Lemon Cumin Aioli

¾ cup mayonnaise

Juice of ½ lemon

Zest of 1 lemon

1 tsp ground cumin

½ tsp black pepper

Kosher salt

Every time I go out to eat and see calamari on a menu, I can't help but order it. Crispy, tender rings of goodness? Sign me up! Contrary to popular belief, calamari is really easy to make at home. Just make sure you get fresh calamari that's on the smaller side, as it tends to be more tender, and have the fishmonger clean them to save you one extra step. Marinating the calamari with punchy flavors really gives it an upgrade from typical restaurant fare and is totally worth the effort!

To make the calamari, place the calamari in a large bowl and add the lemon juice, garlic, ginger, chilis, and salt to taste. Mix well and marinate for 10 minutes at room temperature.

To a large resealable plastic bag, add the flour, cornstarch, baking powder, pepper, and 1 tsp of salt. Seal and shake to mix well.

Add a quarter of the marinated calamari to the bag, seal, and shake to coat. Remove the calamari from the bag, shaking off any excess flour, and lay on a baking sheet in 1 even layer. Working in batches, repeat with the remaining calamari.

Add 3 inches (8 cm) of oil to a large pot or wok on medium-high heat. When the oil reaches 350°F, gently lower the calamari rings in batches, being sure not to crowd the pan. Cook for 3 to 4 minutes, or until golden brown. Drain on a wire rack over a baking sheet.

To make the aioli, add the mayonnaise, lemon juice and zest, cumin, and pepper to a bowl. Season with salt to taste and mix well to combine.

Serve the hot calamari rings with the aioli for dipping.

Tamarind Fish Curry

SERVES 4

2 Tbsp seedless tamarind pulp
  (see note on page 122)

½ cup boiling water

3 Tbsp canola oil

1 tsp fenugreek seeds

5 shallots, thinly sliced

3 cloves garlic, crushed

2 Tbsp curry leaves (optional)

½ Tbsp Kashmiri chili powder

½ Tbsp ground coriander

1 tsp ground fennel seed

1 cup strained tomato sauce
  (passata)

2 cups water

Kosher salt

2 lb (900 g) firm-fleshed fish steaks
  (mackerel, snapper, whiting,
  king fish, blue fish)

Classic Basmati Rice (page 137),
  for serving

Oh how I love tamarind! This tart and sticky fruit is used in so many cuisines around the world, and is popular in South Indian cookery. The sour edge of the tamarind almost acts like citrus in the way that it complements the fish. This recipe is excellent on a weeknight, as the fish takes next to no time to simmer in the curry. I use passata as a shortcut instead of puréeing and straining tomatoes, which saves a lot of time. Be sure to have a big heap of steaming rice to serve this with.

To a small bowl, add the tamarind and top with the boiling water. Soak for 5 minutes. When cool enough to handle, massage the tamarind to release its pulp into the water. Strain the water into a bowl, discarding any fibers or seeds left behind.

To a large pot or Dutch oven on medium heat, add the oil. Once the oil is hot, add the fenugreek seeds and toast for 15 to 20 seconds. Add the shallots, garlic, and curry leaves, and sauté for 4 to 5 minutes, or until softened and translucent.

Add the chili powder, ground coriander, and fennel seed. Toast the spices for 15 to 30 seconds or until fragrant. Pour in the tomato sauce and cook for 10 to 12 minutes on medium-high heat or until the tomatoes reduce by at least half and the fats in the pan begin to sizzle along the edges of the tomato sauce.

Add the water, tamarind water, and salt to taste. Bring to a boil. Gently lower in the fish, and reduce the heat to medium. Cook for 5 to 7 minutes depending on the thickness of the fish, or until opaque and firm.

Serve over hot rice.

Manchurian Shrimp

SERVES 4

For the Shrimp

1½ lb (680 g) peeled and deveined shrimp (size 16/20)

3 Tbsp cornstarch

1 Tbsp grated ginger

2 cloves garlic, finely grated

1 large egg

½ tsp kosher salt

¼ tsp black pepper

Canola oil, for deep frying

For the Sauce

½ cup chicken broth

3 Tbsp strained tomato sauce (passata)

2 Tbsp vinegar- or chili-based hot sauce (Louisiana style or sriracha)

1 Tbsp dark soy sauce

½ tsp kosher salt

1 Tbsp cornstarch

¼ tsp red food coloring

3 Tbsp canola oil

1 Tbsp grated ginger

2 cloves garlic, finely grated

3 Thai green chilis, thinly sliced

½ small yellow onion, finely minced

¼ cup chopped fresh coriander (cilantro), for garnish

Classic Basmati Rice (page 137), for serving

This is easily one of my favorite Indian-Chinese dishes of all time, and the sauce alone has made me scrape the bottom of my plate time and again. Like many Manchurian dishes, the sauce features lots of garlic, ginger, and Thai green chilis, which add to the aroma and heat of this dish. The key to victory with this one is to flash fry the shrimp until they are just cooked through, and toss them in the sauce for just a few seconds before serving to preserve their succulent texture. The result is super-tender shrimp coated in a velvety, savory sauce that pairs extremely well with hot basmati rice.

To make the shrimp, add the shrimp to a large bowl along with the cornstarch, ginger, garlic, egg, salt, and pepper. Mix well to combine.

Add 2 inches (5 cm) of oil to a deep pan on medium-high heat. Add the shrimp pieces one by one, cooking in batches if necessary to avoid crowding the pan. Cook for 2 to 3 minutes, until crispy on the outside and cooked through to the middle. Drain on a paper towel–lined plate.

To make the sauce, add the broth, tomato sauce, hot sauce, soy sauce, salt, cornstarch, and food coloring to a bowl and whisk until smooth.

To another large frying pan on high heat, add the canola oil, followed by the ginger, garlic, chilis, and onions. Sauté for 3 to 4 minutes or until all the ingredients are fragrant and slightly softened.

Whisk together the sauce 1 more time before pouring into the hot pan. Stir continuously, and let the sauce come to a simmer to thicken, 3 to 4 minutes. Once the sauce is glossy and thick, add the fried shrimp and stir to coat.

Garnish with fresh coriander and serve alongside hot basmati rice.

Easy Tandoori Fish

SERVES 4

⅓ cup plain yogurt

Juice of ½ lemon

2 tsp finely grated garlic

2 tsp finely grated ginger

½ Tbsp garam masala

½ Tbsp kasoori methi

2 tsp ground ginger

2 tsp Kashmiri chili powder

½ tsp ground nutmeg

Kosher salt

Red gel food coloring (optional)

4 firm-fleshed fish steaks, about
  2 lb (1 kg) (halibut, grouper,
  mahi-mahi, or salmon)

Restaurant-Style Butter Naan
  (page 164), for serving

Thinly sliced red onions, for serving

4 lemon wedges, for serving

Tandoori chicken was one of the first few recipes I ever posted on YouTube, and it resonated with close to a million people worldwide. While the tandoori marinade is great with chicken, it is also stellar with seafood! I've suggested baking the fish as an easy preparation, but if you have a grill that's ready to be fired up, go for it! Just remember that fish can be delicate, so choosing a firmer variety will be best for this recipe, as it will be less likely to fall apart. Serve this recipe with butter naan, red onions, and wedges of lemon.

Preheat the oven to 500°F. Line a baking sheet with parchment paper.

To a large bowl, add the yogurt, lemon juice, garlic, grated ginger, garam masala, kasoori methi, ground ginger, chili powder, nutmeg, and salt to taste. Mix well to combine. Add a few drops of red gel food coloring and mix until the iconic tandoori red is achieved.

Add the fish steaks to the marinade and mix to coat. Cover and marinate in the fridge for 30 minutes to 1 hour.

Arrange the fish on the prepared baking sheet and bake for 22 to 25 minutes or until slightly charred on the outside and cooked through to the middle. The fish should flake easily.

Serve with naan, onions, and lemon wedges.

Meat

Mint Coriander Lamb Kebabs

SERVES 4

2 lb (900 g) ground lamb

1 small yellow onion, finely minced

½ cup chopped mint leaves

½ cup chopped fresh coriander (cilantro)

5 Thai green chilis, finely minced

3 cloves garlic, finely grated

1 Tbsp finely grated ginger

2 tsp ground coriander

2 tsp ground cumin

Juice of 1 lemon

½ cup melted ghee, divided

3 tsp kosher salt

½ cup plain yogurt

½ cup Mint Coriander Chutney (page 236)

Restaurant-Style Butter Naan (page 164), for serving

Kebabs are often on the menu at my home because they are a quick and easy way to elevate ground meat. While I have suggested lamb for this recipe, feel free to use any meat or ground meat alternative you like. These kebabs have a slight char on the outside, with the vibrant, herby flavors of mint and coriander. The addition of melted ghee in this recipe helps keep the kebabs ultra moist, while giving them a slightly nutty roasted flavor. These kebabs can easily be turned into a delicious wrap by being stuffed into hot Restaurant-Style Butter Naan (page 164).

Soak 8 bamboo skewers in water.

To a large bowl, add the lamb, onion, mint, fresh coriander, chilis, garlic, ginger, ground coriander, cumin, lemon juice, and ¼ cup of the ghee. Season with the salt and mix well to combine. Refrigerate for a minimum of 1 hour to firm up the mixture.

Wet your hands. Take a lemon-sized portion of the kebab mixture and form it into a 3-inch (8 cm) log along the length of the soaked bamboo skewer. Place on a baking sheet. Repeat with the remaining kebab mixture.

Preheat a grill to 425°F. Place the kebabs on the hot grill and cook for 4 to 5 minutes on each side, basting with the remaining ghee, until slightly charred and cooked all the way through to the middle.

Alternatively, pan fry in oil for 3 to 4 minutes until crispy and golden and cooked through to the middle. When cut in the middle, the juices should run clear.

To a small bowl, add the yogurt and mint coriander chutney. Stir together until completely combined.

Serve the kebabs with the sauce and naan.

Pan-Roasted Lamb Chops with Chili Mint Dressing

SERVES 4

12 lamb rib or loin chops
 (about 2 lb/1 kg)

3 tsp cumin

3 tsp black pepper

Kosher salt

3 Tbsp canola oil

¼ cup olive oil

Juice of 1 lemon

3 Tbsp chopped mint leaves

½ long red chili, sliced into
 thin rounds

Coconut Rice (page 145) or
 Mint Rice (page 146), for serving

Kachumber Salad (page 228),
 for serving

Lamb chops are one of my favorite cuts of meat—they are so flavorful and easy to cook, and they're even easier to eat. The beautiful crust of cumin and black pepper on these chops gives them a delightful smoky flavor that is complemented by the heat and tang of the dressing. These chops are great to make when guests are coming over, as they are fast to fry up yet very impressive. Serve them with Coconut Rice (page 145) or Mint Rice (page 146) and Kachumber Salad (page 228) to make it a complete meal. Don't feel shy about eating these with your fingers; they're so good!

Preheat the oven to 450°F.

Season the lamb chops generously on both sides with cumin, pepper, and salt to taste.

Add the canola oil to a large frying pan on high heat. Once hot, gently lower in a few lamb chops, making sure not to crowd the pan. Brown for 2 to 3 minutes on each side, then transfer to a parchment-lined baking sheet. Repeat with the remaining lamb chops.

Transfer the browned lamb chops to the oven and bake for an additional 5 minutes, or until the fat around the perimeter of the lamb chops starts to crisp and the chops are firm but have a slight bounce to the touch. Transfer to a serving platter.

In a small bowl, whisk together the olive oil, lemon juice, mint, chili, and salt to taste.

Pour the chili mint dressing over the lamb chops. Serve hot with coconut rice or mint rice, and kachumber salad.

30-Minute Keema Pav

SERVES 4

For the Keema

3 Tbsp canola oil

1 bay leaf

3 cloves

1 tsp black peppercorns

1 cinnamon stick

1 large yellow onion, finely chopped

2 Tbsp kasoori methi

5 Thai green chilis, split lengthwise

5 cloves garlic, finely grated

1 Tbsp finely grated ginger

4 Tbsp butter (salted or unsalted)

½ cup finely chopped fresh
  coriander (cilantro)

½ cup finely chopped mint leaves

2 large tomatoes, finely diced

1 tsp Kashmiri chili powder

½ tsp ground turmeric

2 lb (900 g) ground lamb (or chicken)

Kosher salt

2 cups water

For Assembly

8 burger or brioche buns

¼ cup melted butter

½ cup chopped sweet onions

¼ cup chopped fresh coriander
  (cilantro)

Whenever I describe keema pav, I cannot help but refer to it as the Indian version of sloppy Joes. Saucy spiced ground meat tucked away in butter-toasted buns. The ideal weeknight meal, as it comes together as quickly as, if not faster than, a Bolognese sauce. This is the sandwich that eats like a meal, so don't hesitate to heap on the keema, and have extra buns on the side for scooping.

To make the keema, add the oil to a large frying pan on medium heat. Add the bay leaf, cloves, peppercorns, and cinnamon and cook for 10 to 15 seconds or until the cloves have puffed up. Add the onion and cook for 5 to 6 minutes or until softened and golden. Add the kasoori methi, chilis, garlic, and ginger, and sauté for 30 seconds or until fragrant.

Add the butter to the pan followed by the fresh coriander and mint. Sauté for 15 seconds to soften the herbs. Increase the heat to medium-high and add the tomatoes. Cook the tomatoes for 10 to 12 minutes, stirring occasionally, until they become jammy in texture and the fats in the pan begin to sizzle along the edges of the tomatoes. Sprinkle in the chili powder and turmeric, and stir to mix.

Increase the heat to high and add the lamb and salt to taste. Stir the lamb into the tomato mixture and cook, stirring continuously, until the lamb has cooked through and any excess moisture in the pan has evaporated. Add the water and cook until a bubbly, saucy curry forms.

To assemble, brush the burger buns with butter on both sides and toast in a hot pan until golden on both sides. Serve the keema alongside the buns garnished with onions and fresh coriander. Alternatively, stuff the buns with the keema mixture and serve as a sandwich.

Note: Any leftover keema mixture can be stored in a covered container in the fridge for up to 3 days. Alternatively, portion the keema into freezer-safe resealable bags, spread flat, seal, and freeze. The frozen keema will keep for up to 6 months.

Lamb Karahi

SERVES 4

1½ lb (680 g) lamb leg or shoulder, cut into small pieces (bone-in or boneless)

5 cloves garlic, finely grated

2 Tbsp finely grated ginger

1 Tbsp cumin seeds

1 Tbsp coriander seeds

3 tsp black peppercorns

4 green cardamom pods

4 dried red chilis

1 tsp garam masala

1 tsp ground turmeric

½ cup canola oil

1 large yellow onion, thinly sliced

2 large tomatoes, finely chopped

¼ cup plain yogurt, whisked

Kosher salt

1 Tbsp kasoori methi

2-inch (5 cm) knob ginger, peeled and julienned

½ cup chopped fresh coriander (cilantro)

2 long green chilis, split lengthwise

Classic Basmati Rice (page 137), for serving

Kulchas (page 172), for serving

Cucumber Pomegranate Raita (page 228), for serving

A karahi or kadai is a round, deep pot in which this curry is typically cooked. Don't worry if you don't have one, as a large wok or pot will work just fine. The curry is rich and deep in flavor, thanks to the combination of the freshly ground spices, caramelized onions, and tangy yogurt, and the lamb becomes so tender that it can be eaten with a spoon. The additions of fresh zippy ginger and fresh green chilis at the end really amplify this curry. This recipe is a great introduction to cooking lamb curries, as it has only a handful of steps while delivering authentic flavor.

To a medium pot, add the lamb, garlic, and ginger. Add enough water to just barely cover the lamb. Bring to a boil, then reduce the heat to low. Cover and simmer for 1½ hours or until fork tender. Alternatively, place the lamb, garlic, ginger, and water in a multi-cooker or pressure cooker, and cook for 25 minutes on high pressure, then let the pressure release naturally. Remove the meat and transfer to a bowl. Reserve ½ cup of the cooking liquid.

To a small blender or coffee grinder, add the cumin seeds, coriander seeds, peppercorns, cardamom, red chilis, garam masala, and turmeric. Pulse to form a coarse powder.

To a large pot on medium-high heat, add the oil. Once hot, add the onion and sauté, stirring occasionally, until deeply browned, about 15 minutes. Add the tomatoes and cook until jammy and soft, 10 to 12 minutes.

Add the ground spices and sauté for 1 minute or until fragrant. Add the cooked lamb and ½ cup of the cooking liquid. Stir to combine and bring to a simmer.

Reduce the heat to low, then slowly add the whisked yogurt, stirring continuously to incorporate it into the sauce. Season with salt to taste. Increase the heat to medium and continue cooking for 10 minutes to reduce the sauce until it has thickened slightly. Remove from the heat and sprinkle over the kasoori methi, julienned ginger, fresh coriander, and green chilis. Mix to combine.

Serve with hot rice, kulchas, and/or cucumber pomegranate raita.

Sticky Tamarind Date Ribs

SERVES 4 TO 6

¼ cup packed brown sugar

1 Tbsp kosher salt

2 tsp garam masala

2 tsp cayenne chili powder

1 tsp garlic powder

1 tsp black pepper

2 sides of baby back ribs
(about 4 lb/2 kg)

1 cup chicken broth

¼ cup seedless tamarind pulp
(see note)

6 medjool dates, pitted

1 cup boiling water

½ cup finely chopped or
powdered jaggery (see note)

3 tsp ground cumin

1 tsp Kashmiri chili powder

½ cup ketchup

3-Ingredient Peas Pulao (page 138),
for serving

This recipe takes inspiration from my favorite 4-Ingredient Tamarind Chutney (page 231), which I like to serve with many Indian fried appetizers. Tamarind has a beautiful fruity, tart flavor that works well to cut richness, which is why it complements ribs perfectly. If you are new to preparing ribs, this recipe takes all the guesswork out of it. Baking the ribs gets them nice and tender without having to monitor their doneness on a grill. To make it a meal, serve them up with a side of 3-Ingredient Peas Pulao (page 138).

Preheat the oven to 250°F.

To a small bowl, add the brown sugar, salt, garam masala, chili powder, garlic powder, and pepper. Mix well to combine.

Rub the spice mixture on both sides of the ribs, and place the ribs on a large baking sheet. Pour the chicken broth around the ribs, and cover with aluminum foil. Seal the edges to keep the steam from escaping as the ribs bake. Bake for 2 hours. After removing the baked ribs from the oven, increase the oven temperature to 450°F.

Add the tamarind and dates to a small bowl and top with the boiling water. After 10 minutes, transfer the tamarind and water to a blender and blend until smooth. Strain through a sieve, discarding any pulp or fibers left behind.

Transfer the puréed tamarind to a saucepan, and add the jaggery, cumin, chili powder, and ketchup. Simmer for 10 to 12 minutes or until the sauce has thickened.

Remove the ribs from the baking sheet and discard any remaining liquid. Brush the ribs generously with the tamarind sauce. Return to the oven and bake for an additional 10 minutes or until browned and glossy. Alternatively, place the ribs on a 400°F grill for 3 to 4 minutes on each side to char slightly.

Cut the ribs between the bones to serve.

Notes:
1. Seedless tamarind is soft and comes packed in small rectangles at most Asian grocery stores.
2. Jaggery is an unrefined sugar made from cane sugar. It has deep caramel and molasses notes, and can typically be purchased in small blocks or powdered at Asian grocery stores.

Goan Pork Vindaloo

SERVES 4

2 Tbsp Kashmiri chili powder (see note)

1 tsp black mustard seeds

1 tsp black peppercorns

1 tsp cumin seeds

2 tsp coriander seeds

½ tsp fenugreek seeds

1 cinnamon stick

4 cloves

⅓ cup apple cider vinegar

1 long red chili, roughly chopped

8 cloves garlic

2-inch (5 cm) knob ginger, roughly chopped

2 tsp white sugar

2 lb (900 g) boneless pork butt or shoulder, cut into 2-inch (5 cm) chunks

½ cup canola oil

2 medium yellow onions, finely chopped

3 cups water

Kosher salt

Classic Basmati Rice (page 137), for serving

Restaurant-Style Butter Naan (page 164), for serving

Hailing from the state of Goa, vindaloo is often featured on Indian restaurant menus as the spicy curry option. However, over time I've realized that it's okay to temper the heat of a vindaloo so that it has just enough kick without setting my mouth on fire. This recipe is especially easy since the marinade for the pork is mixed in a blender and also becomes the base for the sauce as the pork is cooked.

To a small blender or coffee grinder, add the chili powder, mustard seeds, peppercorns, cumin seeds, coriander seeds, fenugreek seeds, cinnamon, and cloves. Process until a fine powder forms and add to a large bowl.

To the same blender, add the vinegar, chili, garlic, ginger, and sugar. Blend until smooth. Pour this mixture over the ground spices and mix to form a paste. Add the pork and mix to coat.

To a deep pot on medium-high heat, add the oil. Once hot, add the onions and sauté for 5 to 6 minutes or until softened and golden brown.

Increase the heat to high and add the pork. Mix the pork into the onions, and cook for 5 minutes, or until the pork slightly firms up and turns opaque in color.

Add the water and season with salt to taste. Bring up to a simmer. Cook for 1½ hours or until the pork is fork tender and the sauce has reduced and thickened. Alternatively, cook the mixture in a multi-cooker or pressure cooker for 30 minutes on high pressure until fork tender, then let the pressure release naturally. Set to sauté mode if using a multi-cooker, or return to a simmer on medium-high heat if using a pressure cooker, and reduce the sauce until thickened.

Serve with hot basmati rice or naan.

Note: If you really want to go for it, swap the Kashmiri chili powder for an equal amount of cayenne chili powder for extra fire.

The Ultimate Indian Lamb Burgers

SERVES 4

For the Lamb Burgers

1 Tbsp canola oil

1 small yellow onion, minced

1 long red chili, seeded and minced

4 cloves garlic, finely minced

1 Tbsp finely grated ginger

2 lb (900 g) ground lamb

½ cup chopped fresh coriander (cilantro)

2 tsp garam masala

1 tsp Kashmiri chili powder

1 tsp ground fennel seed

½ tsp ground turmeric

3 tsp kosher salt

For Assembly

4 burger buns

2 Tbsp melted butter

1 head Bibb lettuce

1 beefsteak tomato, thinly sliced

1 red onion, thinly sliced

Cucumber Pomegranate Raita (page 228)

When I'm looking to indulge in a burger, this is what I reach for. The hot spiced lamb patty paired with the cooling raita is a classic combo that works so well in between burger buns. Juicy, spicy, cool, and fresh! Serve with French fries dusted with cayenne chili powder and salt to make the ultimate takeout combo at home.

To make the burgers, to a frying pan on medium heat, add the oil. Once hot, add the onion and chili, and sauté for 3 to 4 minutes or until softened and translucent. Add the garlic and ginger and warm through for 15 to 20 seconds. Transfer to a plate and allow to cool.

Add the ground lamb to a large bowl followed by the cooled onion mixture, fresh coriander, garam masala, chili powder, ground fennel seed, turmeric, and salt. Mix well to combine. Refrigerate for 30 minutes to firm up the meat.

Divide the burger mixture into 4 equal portions and form into patties. Preheat the barbecue to 400°F. Grill for 3 to 4 minutes on each side or until slightly charred on the outside and cooked through to the middle. Alternatively, pan fry in a little bit of oil for 2 to 3 minutes on each side until browned on both sides and cooked through to the middle.

To assemble, brush the burger buns with butter and toast in a pan until golden.

Place a piece of Bibb lettuce and a slice of tomato on the bottom bun and top with a lamb burger patty. Place a slice of red onion on top and a spoonful of raita, and sandwich with the top bun. Serve with extra raita on the side for dipping.

Cheesy Keema Quesadillas

SERVES 4

2 Tbsp canola oil

1 medium yellow onion, finely chopped

3 cloves garlic, finely grated

½ Tbsp finely grated ginger

1 lb (450 g) ground lamb

1 tsp Kashmiri chili powder

1 tsp ground cumin

1 tsp ground coriander

1 tsp black pepper

Kosher salt

6 cups grated Tex-Mex cheese

8 medium flour tortilas

1 cup thinly sliced sweet white onions

2 jalapeño peppers, thinly sliced

½ cup chopped fresh coriander (cilantro)

Mint Coriander Chutney (page 236), for serving

Mexican hot sauce, for serving

Sour cream, for serving

This recipe was born when I happened to have leftover keema (ground meat curry) in the fridge. I was getting bored eating it just as it was, so I stuffed it in a tortilla, sprinkled on some cheese, and one of my favorite Indian/Tex-Mex mash-ups came to life! Feel free to swap out the keema for any thick curry dish (vegetarian or non-vegetarian) that you may have crowding your fridge! This is an easy recipe to pull off any night of the week, as the ground lamb takes next to no time to cook.

To a large frying pan on medium heat, add the oil. Once hot, add the yellow onion and sauté for 3 to 4 minutes or until softened and translucent. Add the garlic and ginger, and cook for 30 seconds or until fragrant.

Increase the heat to high and add the lamb. Cook for 8 to 10 minutes, stirring and breaking up the lamb with a spoon, until all the moisture has evaporated from the pan and the lamb begins to brown. Add the chili powder, cumin, ground coriander, pepper, and salt to taste. Sauté for 30 seconds to toast the spices.

To assemble, sprinkle a heaping ¼ cup of cheese onto one half of the tortilla. Then top with one-eighth of the lamb, ⅛ cup white onions, 1 Tbsp of jalapeños, and 1 Tbsp fresh coriander. Sprinkle another heaping ¼ cup of cheese on top, and fold over the other side of the tortilla. Repeat with the remaining tortillas and fillings.

Place 2 quesadillas in a large pan on medium-high heat and toast for 3 to 4 minutes on each side until golden brown and the cheese has melted. Place the warmed quesadillas on a baking sheet and repeat with the remaining quesadillas, cooking in batches.

Serve with mint coriander chutney, hot sauce, and sour cream.

Chettinad Mutton Sukka Varuval
Mutton Fry

1½ lb (680 g) boneless lamb
    shoulder or leg, cut into
    ½-inch (1.5 cm) cubes

¾ cup water

1 tsp ground turmeric

4 cloves garlic, finely grated

½ Tbsp finely grated ginger

Kosher salt

3 Tbsp canola oil

2 tsp fennel seeds

1 medium yellow onion,
    finely chopped

3 tsp cayenne chili powder

3 tsp ground coriander

1 medium tomato, finely chopped

¼ cup fresh curry leaves

3-Ingredient Peas Pulao (page 138),
    for serving

5-Ingredient Chapatis (page 168),
    for serving

I was around nine years old when I went to India on vacation and had my first taste of takeout mutton fry, brought home piping hot wrapped in a small banana leaf parcel. The smell was absolutely intoxicating. The tiny pieces of lamb were tender and clung to the dry spiced sauce beautifully. While you can leave the curry leaves out of this recipe, I do recommend making the extra effort to find them, as they add an undeniable perfume that will transport you to South India. Using a multi-cooker or pressure cooker to cook the lamb is a time saver here, and results in the most tender melt-in-your-mouth meat. This is delicious served with 3-Ingredient Peas Pulao (page 138) and 5-Ingredient Chapatis (page 168) for scooping.

Add the lamb to a multi-cooker or pressure cooker along with the water, turmeric, garlic, ginger, and salt to taste. Pressure cook on high for 25 to 30 minutes or until very tender. Let the pressure release naturally.

Add the oil to a medium pot on medium-high heat. Once hot, add the fennel seeds and toast for 10 seconds. Add the onion and sauté for 5 to 6 minutes or until softened and slightly golden. Add the chili powder and ground coriander and toast the spices for 10 to 15 seconds. Add the tomato and cook, stirring occasionally, until jammy in texture.

Add the cooked lamb with its cooking liquid to the pot. Season with salt to taste, and cook on high heat, stirring often, until the liquid has completely reduced and the lamb starts to crackle in the pan. Add the curry leaves and cook for 15 to 20 seconds.

Serve hot with peas pulao and/or chapatis.

Lamb Rogan Josh

SERVES 4

1½ lb (680 g) cubed lamb leg
  or shoulder

2 tsp garam masala

2 tsp ground fennel seed

1 Tbsp + 1 tsp Kashmiri red chili
  powder, divided

1 Tbsp + 2 tsp finely grated garlic,
  divided

1 Tbsp + 2 tsp finely grated ginger,
  divided

2¼ cups plain yogurt, divided

Kosher salt

½ cup canola oil, divided

2 tsp fennel seeds

2 tsp black peppercorns

2 black cardamom pods

6 green cardamom pods

4 cloves

1 cinnamon stick

1 large yellow onion, thinly sliced

3 cups water

Kulchas (page 172), for serving

3-Ingredient Peas Pulao (page 138),
  for serving

If you've been to an Indian restaurant, chances are that you've seen lamb rogan josh as the signature lamb curry on the menu. Thought to have originated in Kashmir, this curry is mild and mellow, focusing more on the flavor of whole spices while chili takes a back seat. I particularly like using bone-in lamb for this recipe as it creates depth of flavor; however, don't hesitate to go boneless if that's easier. Marinating the lamb with yogurt and spices helps tenderize and flavor the meat even before the cooking process begins. This recipe is delicious simply served with kulchas and peas pulao.

To a bowl, add the lamb, garam masala, ground fennel seed, 1 tsp chili powder, 2 tsp garlic, 2 tsp ginger, ¼ cup yogurt, and salt to taste. Mix well to combine, cover, and refrigerate for a minimum of 30 minutes to overnight.

Add ¼ cup of the oil to a large Dutch oven on medium-high heat. Once hot, add the lamb and cook it for 15 to 20 minutes or until browned on all sides. Transfer the lamb to a bowl.

Reduce the heat to medium and add the remaining ¼ cup of oil. Add the fennel seeds, peppercorns, black cardamom pods, green cardamom pods, cloves, and cinnamon stick. Toast for 15 to 20 seconds. Add the onions and cook for 10 minutes, until softened and browned. Add the remaining 1 Tbsp garlic and the remaining 1 Tbsp ginger and cook for 1 minute.

Return the reserved lamb and any juices that may have accumulated back to the pot. Reduce the heat to low and whisk the remaining 2 cups of yogurt until smooth. Slowly add the yogurt to the lamb, stirring well to combine.

Add the water, remaining 1 Tbsp chili powder, and salt to taste. Cook, partially covered, on medium-low heat for 1½ hours or until the lamb is tender and the sauce has thickened. Alternatively, place the lamb in a multi-cooker or pressure cooker and cook on high pressure for 30 minutes or until fork tender. Let the pressure release naturally. Then change the setting to sauté mode, if using a multi-cooker, or bring to a simmer on medium-high heat if using a pressure cooker, and reduce the sauce until it has thickened.

Serve with kulchas or peas pulao.

Rice
and
Grains

Classic Basmati Rice

MAKES 6 CUPS

2 cups basmati rice

I questioned whether this recipe was too simple to feature, but I know what a struggle it can be to get rice right! Follow this technique, and you will have beautiful long grains of unbroken rice every single time, I promise.

Place the rice in a bowl and cover with lukewarm water. Gently massage the grains until the water turns cloudy. Drain the water and repeat the process until the water runs clear. Soak for 30 minutes.

Bring a large pot of water to a rolling boil. Drain the soaked rice in a colander and add the rice to the boiling water. Stir and boil for 5 to 6 minutes or until the rice is tender but still has a little bit of bite.

Drain the rice in a colander and let it sit for 10 minutes, then transfer to a serving dish.

Store any leftover rice in an airtight container in the fridge for up to 4 days.

3-Ingredient Peas Pulao

SERVES 4 TO 6

2 cups basmati rice
1 cup frozen green peas
2 Tbsp canola oil
1 Tbsp cumin seeds

When I am making a variety of curries for a dinner party and want to upgrade my basmati rice with minimal effort, I make this peas pulao. It only takes three ingredients and is so simple to put together. The tiny pops of green from the sweet peas make the rice more lively, while the crunch of the cumin seeds adds lovely textural contrast.

Place the rice in a bowl and cover with lukewarm water. Gently massage the grains until the water turns cloudy. Drain the water and repeat the process until the water runs clear. Soak for 30 minutes, then drain in a colander.

Bring a large pot of water to a rolling boil and add the drained rice. Stir and boil for 4 to 5 minutes, or until the rice still has a bit of bite. Add the frozen peas and stir, allowing them to warm through for 1 minute.

Drain the rice and peas and let them cool in the colander for 5 minutes, then transfer to a large baking sheet and spread out into 1 even layer (see note).

To a small saucepan on medium heat, add the oil. Once the oil is hot, add the cumin seeds and toast for 15 to 20 seconds.

Pour the hot cumin and oil all over the rice. Then using a spoon or your hands, gently mix the rice to mix in the cumin.

Transfer to a plate to serve. Store leftovers in an airtight container in the fridge for up to 4 days.

 Note: Cooling the rice helps ensure the grains don't break when the hot spiced oil is mixed in at the end.

Thayir Sadam
Curd Rice

SERVES 4

1½ cups basmati rice

Kosher salt

2 cups whole milk

1 cup plain yogurt

1 Thai green chili, seeded and
   thinly sliced

1-inch (2.5 cm) knob ginger,
   finely grated

½ cup peeled and chopped green
   mango (see note on page 227)

½ Tbsp canola oil

1 tsp black mustard seeds

1 tsp skinless urad dhal (black gram)
   (see note)

2 Tbsp chopped fresh coriander
   (cilantro)

Wedding Mango Pickle (page 227),
   for serving

Note: Urad dhal can be purchased
in many different forms: whole
with skin, whole skinless, and split
skinless. For this recipe, feel free
to use whole or split skinless.

In its simplest form, thayir sadam is a dish of rice mashed together with yogurt and salt until creamy in texture. It can be served on its own or accompanied by Indian pickles (for a pop of heat and acidity), curries (to make a substantial meal), or fresh mango (if you like the combo of sweet and savory). The version I'm sharing is most often served at South Indian weddings and features tempered spices and fresh green mango for bursts of crunch and tang. I personally love eating it with Wedding Mango Pickle (page 227) as an accompaniment, or with Tamarind Fish Curry (page 107) to make a hearty meal.

Place the rice in a bowl and cover with lukewarm water. Gently massage the grains until the water turns cloudy. Drain the water and repeat the process until the water runs clear. Soak for 30 minutes, then drain in a colander.

Bring a large pot of water to a rolling boil and add the drained rice. Cook, uncovered, for 10 minutes, or until very tender. Drain, then transfer to a large bowl. Season with salt to taste and stir with a large spoon, intentionally breaking the grains of rice until creamy in texture.

Add the milk to a saucepan, bring it to a boil, and then immediately remove it from the heat. Pour the milk over the rice and mix until well combined. Pour the rice onto a baking sheet and spread into 1 even layer. Allow to completely cool to room temperature.

Add the yogurt and sliced chilis to the cooled rice. Take the grated ginger and squeeze over the rice, extracting as much juice as you can and discarding any fibers left behind. Stir to combine, then stir in the green mango.

Add the oil to a small saucepan, and heat on medium. Once hot, add the mustard seeds. Once they start to pop, add the urad dhal and wait for it to turn golden, about 20 seconds. Immediately pour the spiced oil over the rice and mix to combine.

Stir in the fresh coriander and transfer to a bowl. Enjoy at room temperature or chilled with mango pickle.

Tomato Rice

SERVES 4 TO 6

1 Tbsp canola oil

1 Tbsp ghee

1 cinnamon stick

3 green cardamom pods

3 cloves

1 star anise

1 bay leaf

1 large yellow onion, thinly sliced

4 Thai green chilis, cut lengthwise

4 cloves garlic, finely grated

1-inch (2.5 cm) knob ginger, finely grated

2 large tomatoes, chopped

Kosher salt

½ cup frozen green peas

2 Tbsp chopped fresh coriander (cilantro)

2 Tbsp chopped fresh mint

6 cups cooked and cooled Classic Basmati Rice (page 137)

2-Ingredient Onion Pachadi, for serving (page 238)

Appalams (or pappadams), for serving (see note)

Now that you have learned the art of preparing Classic Basmati Rice (page 137), it is so easy to transform it into a multitude of rice dishes. The base of this tomato rice is a rich spiced tomato sauce flavored with whole spices, chilis, and herbs, that is then folded into cooked basmati rice. Like many South Indian rice dishes, this one can be served at room temperature. Tomato rice is delicious served with 2-Ingredient Onion Pachadi (page 238) and appalams (or pappadams) as an accompaniment.

To a large pot on medium heat, add the oil and ghee. Once hot, add the cinnamon, cardamom, cloves, star anise, and bay leaf. Toast the spices for 15 to 20 seconds or until fragrant. Add the onion, chilis, garlic, and ginger. Sauté the onion for 4 to 5 minutes or until soft and translucent.

Add the tomatoes and season with salt to taste. Increase the heat to high, and cook for 7 to 8 minutes, or until the tomatoes are soft but haven't completely broken down. Stir in the frozen peas and warm through for 1 to 2 minutes.

Remove from the heat and stir in the fresh coriander and mint. Add the cooled rice to the pot, and gently fold into the sauce, being careful not to break the grains. Continue folding until all the rice takes on an even reddish hue.

Serve warm or at room temperature with onion pachadi and appalams (or pappadams).

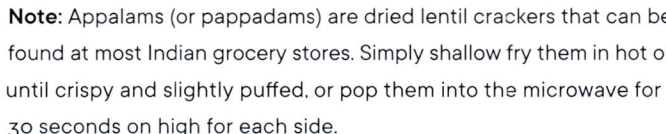

Note: Appalams (or pappadams) are dried lentil crackers that can be found at most Indian grocery stores. Simply shallow fry them in hot oil until crispy and slightly puffed, or pop them into the microwave for 30 seconds on high for each side.

Coconut Rice

SERVES 4 TO 6

1 Tbsp canola oil

2 tsp black mustard seeds

2 tsp skinless urad dhal (black gram)

3 dried red chilis, each broken
  into 3 or 4 pieces

¼ cup curry leaves

¼ tsp asafoetida

2 cups fresh or frozen
  grated coconut

6 cups cooked and cooled
  Classic Basmati Rice (page 137)

Kosher salt

Any opportunity I have to cook with coconut, I take! The nutty tropical note of the coconut in this rice is so delicious paired with the toasty tempered spices. The key is to use fresh or frozen coconut for this recipe, as dried will not provide the correct flavor or texture. While coconut rice is typically eaten on its own or amongst a selection of other rice dishes (like tomato rice or mint rice), I personally like serving it with Pan-Roasted Lamb Chops with Chili Mint Dressing (page 116).

To a large wok or frying pan on medium heat, add the oil. Once hot, add the mustard seeds and let them crackle for 10 to 15 seconds. Add the urad dhal and toast for 20 seconds or until slightly golden.

Add the chilis, curry leaves, and asafoetida, and sauté for 10 seconds or until fragrant. The chilis should maintain their bright red color and should not brown. Add the coconut and cook, stirring often, until the coconut becomes dry in texture but does not brown, 2 to 3 minutes.

Add the cooled rice and season with salt to taste. Mix gently into the coconut and spices, and warm through. Serve warm or at room temperature.

Mint Rice

SERVES 4 TO 6

2 Tbsp seedless tamarind pulp (see note on page 122)

4 Tbsp boiling water

4 Tbsp canola oil, divided

3 dried red chilis, broken into small pieces

½ tsp asafoetida

2 cups mint leaves

Kosher salt

6 cups cooked and cooled Classic Basmati Rice (page 137)

While mint is typically used in its fresh form in most dishes around the world, it also has the capacity to take on an herbal tea-like flavor when cooked. Paired with tart tamarind and chili in this recipe, the result is a beautifully perfumed rice with an herby and vibrant flavor profile. Though not traditional, this recipe would pair wonderfully with Hariyali Spatchcock Roast Chicken (page 75).

Add the tamarind to a small bowl and top with the boiling water. Soak for 10 minutes or until soft.

To a frying pan on medium heat, add 2 Tbsp of the oil. Once hot, add the chilis and asafoetida, and cook for 10 seconds or until fragrant. The chilis should not brown. Add the mint, and cook for 15 to 30 seconds or until vibrant in color.

Allow the mixture to cool slightly before adding it to a blender with the soaked tamarind (including the soaking liquid), and salt to taste. Blend until a smooth paste forms.

Spread the rice onto a baking sheet. Pour the mint paste over the rice along with the remaining 2 Tbsp of oil. Gently stir and mix, being careful not to break the grains of rice, until the rice takes on a uniform green hue.

Serve at room temperature.

20-Minute Vegetable Upma

SERVES 4

2 cups coarse semolina

⅛ cup canola oil

⅛ cup ghee

2 tsp black mustard seeds

1 Tbsp chana dhal
  (dried split chickpeas)

1 Tbsp skinless urad dhal
  (black gram)

1 medium yellow onion,
  finely chopped

½ tsp asafoetida

1 Tbsp finely chopped ginger

2 Thai green chilis, minced

6 cups water

Kosher salt

½ cup chopped carrots

½ cup frozen green peas

¼ cup chopped fresh coriander
  (cilantro)

5-Minute Coconut Chutney
  (page 232), for serving

Semolina is a form of coarse wheat flour that is revered in Indian cooking for its versatility and heartiness. While it comes in many varieties (superfine, fine, and coarse), be sure to use coarse semolina in this recipe, as the grains will be more distinct and create a fluffier texture. Upma is a dish of aromatics like ginger and green chilis cooked together with vegetables and semolina to create a texture similar to that of fine couscous. It is hearty yet light and delicious partnered with 5-Minute Coconut Chutney (page 232).

To a frying pan on medium-high heat, add the semolina. Toast for 1 to 2 minutes or until slightly nutty in fragrance, but not browned. Transfer to a bowl.

To a large pot on medium heat, add the oil and ghee. Once hot, add the mustard seeds and let them crackle for 10 to 15 seconds. Add the chana dhal and urad dhal, and toast until slightly golden. Add the onion and asafoetida, and sauté the onion until it is soft and translucent. Sprinkle in the ginger and chilis, and sauté for 15 seconds or until fragrant.

Pour in the water and increase the heat to high. Once at a rolling boil, season with salt to taste, and add the carrots and peas. Cook the vegetables until the carrots are tender but still have a bit of bite, about 7 to 8 minutes.

Turn the heat off and begin to slowly scatter the semolina into the water, stirring continuously until smooth. Return to medium heat and cook for 6 to 7 minutes, until the mixture has thickened considerably.

Remove from the heat and stir in the fresh coriander. Serve hot with coconut chutney.

Vegetable Pulao

SERVES 4 TO 6

2 cups basmati rice

2 Tbsp canola oil

2 Tbsp ghee

1 bay leaf

4 cloves

4 green cardamom pods

1 cinnamon stick

1 medium yellow onion,
  finely chopped

2 cloves garlic, minced

1 Tbsp grated ginger

3 Thai green chilis, thinly sliced

2 cups canned coconut milk

2 cups water

Kosher salt

½ cup sliced carrot rounds

½ cup chopped (1¼-inch/3 cm
  pieces) green beans

½ cup frozen peas

½ cup frozen lima beans

¼ cup chopped fresh coriander
  (cilantro)

¼ cup chopped mint

2-Ingredient Onion Pachadi
  (page 238), for serving

This pulao is one of my favorite vegetarian rice dishes! The warmth of the whole spices and the creamy, nutty coconut milk absorb into every single grain of rice in the pot, making it ultra delicious. Also, it's the perfect recipe to use up any hearty veggies you have hanging out in the crisper or freezer. This dish is traditionally served with 2-Ingredient Onion Pachadi (page 238), but would also be delicious with South Indian Egg Masala (page 83) to make a more substantial meal.

Place the rice in a bowl and cover with lukewarm water. Gently massage the grains until the water turns cloudy. Drain the water and repeat the process until the water runs clear. Soak for 30 minutes, then drain in a colander.

To a medium pot on medium heat, add the oil and ghee. Once hot, add the bay leaf, cloves, cardamom, and cinnamon. Sauté the spices for 15 to 20 seconds or until fragrant. Add the onion, garlic, ginger, and chilis, and sauté for 7 to 8 minutes or until the onion is soft and slightly golden.

Pour in the coconut milk and water, and season with salt to taste. Bring to a simmer. Add the carrots, green beans, peas, and lima beans, and cook just until the carrots are tender, 4 to 5 minutes.

Add the drained rice, fresh coriander, and mint, and stir gently for 7 to 8 minutes to thicken without breaking the grains. Cover the pot with aluminum foil and a lid and cook on low heat for 10 minutes.

Remove the pot from the heat and rest for 5 minutes before serving with onion pachadi.

South Indian Lamb Biryani

SERVES 4 TO 6

2 cups basmati rice

1½ lb (680 g) lamb shoulder,
   cut into 1½-inch (4 cm) cubes

6 cloves garlic, finely grated

2-inch (5 cm) knob ginger,
   finely grated

3 cups water, divided

Kosher salt

¼ cup ghee

1 cinnamon stick

2 bay leaves

2 star anise

5 cloves

6 green cardamom pods

1 large yellow onion, finely chopped

6 Thai green chilis, finely minced

¼ cup plain yogurt, whisked

½ cup fresh mint leaves

½ cup fresh coriander (cilantro),
   stems and leaves

Juice of 1 lemon

1 large tomato, cut into big chunks

2-Ingredient Onion Pachadi
   (page 238), for serving

When I am asked what my favorite meal in the world is, the answer is always my mom's biryani. I've had so many variations of this Indian staple in my life, but my mom's recipe is the one that I come back to time and time again. As a kid, and even as an adult, the best part about the entire process for me is removing the lid of the biryani once it's ready and basking in its aroma. This biryani is made with whole spices like cinnamon, star anise, and cloves, which beautifully perfume the rice and the lamb. Comfort food at its best.

Place the rice in a bowl and cover with lukewarm water. Gently massage the grains until the water turns cloudy. Drain the water and repeat the process until the water runs clear. Soak for 30 minutes, then drain and set aside.

Add the lamb to a multi-cooker or pressure cooker with the garlic, ginger, 1 cup of the water, and salt to taste. Seal the multi-cooker. Cook on high pressure for 25 minutes, then let the pressure release naturally. Separate the lamb from the cooking liquid, and set both aside.

To a large pot or Dutch oven on medium heat, add the ghee. Once the ghee is hot, add the cinnamon, bay leaves, star anise, cloves, and cardamom. Sauté for 30 to 45 seconds, until the spices are fragrant or the cloves have puffed up.

Increase the heat to medium-high and add the onion and chilis. Sauté for 5 minutes or until the onions are soft, translucent, and golden.

Add the lamb back to the pot and add the yogurt. Stir continuously to mix the yogurt evenly into the lamb and onions. Pour the reserved cooking liquid into the pot, followed by the remaining 2 cups water. Season with salt to taste.

recipe continues

Add the mint and fresh coriander to a blender with the lemon juice, and blend until coarsely ground. Add this mixture to the pot and stir through. Add the tomato and bring the mixture to a simmer. Once bubbling, add the drained rice to the pot and stir well. Reduce the heat to low and cover the pot with a piece of aluminum foil and a lid to trap the steam.

Cook for 12 to 15 minutes or until the rice has completely absorbed all the liquid in the pot. Remove from the heat and rest for 5 minutes before serving.

Serve with onion pachadi on the side.

Hyderabadi Chicken Biryani

SERVES 4 TO 6

For the Chicken

3 lb (1.4 kg) mixed chicken pieces (drumsticks, thighs, bone-in breast cut into 3 pieces)

½ cup plain yogurt

4 cloves garlic, finely grated

1 Tbsp finely grated ginger

4 Thai green chilis, minced

¼ cup chopped fresh coriander (cilantro)

¼ cup chopped mint

Juice of 1 lemon

1 tsp ground cumin

1 tsp ground coriander

1 tsp Kashmiri chili powder

Kosher salt

For the Fried Onions

1 large sweet onion, thinly sliced

1 Tbsp all-purpose flour

Canola oil, for frying

For the Rice

2 cups basmati rice

2 tsp kosher salt

1 bay leaf

4 cloves

4 green cardamom pods

1 black cardamom pod

1 star anise

1 tsp cumin seeds

1 cinnamon stick

From state to state, city to city, and even village to village in India, the preparation of biryani can vary. It's always hotly debated as to what constitutes a "true" biryani, but in reality they're all authentic in their own way. This variation features the layering method, with the meat being cooked under the rice before being gently folded together at the end. The addition of steeped saffron adds a beautiful aroma to the rice, and even though it's pricey, a tiny bit goes a long way. I like serving this biryani with equal parts Mint Coriander Chutney (page 236) and plain yogurt mixed into one another as a refreshing herby condiment.

To make the chicken, in a large bowl, add the chicken, yogurt, garlic, ginger, chilis, fresh coriander, mint, lemon juice, ground cumin, ground coriander, chili powder, and salt to taste. Mix well to combine. Cover and refrigerate for a minimum of 1 hour to overnight.

To make the fried onions, place the onions in a medium bowl, sprinkle the flour overtop, and mix well to coat. Heat 1 inch (2.5 cm) of oil in a large frying pan on medium-high heat. Cook the onions in batches to not overcrowd the pan for 10 to 12 minutes or until crispy and deeply browned. Drain onto a paper towel–lined plate.

To make the rice, place the rice in a bowl and cover with lukewarm water. Gently massage the grains until the water turns cloudy. Drain the water and repeat the process until the water runs clear. Soak for 30 minutes, then drain in a colander.

Preheat the oven to 425°F.

To cook the rice, bring a large pot of water to a rolling boil. Add the salt, bay leaf, cloves, green cardamom pods, black cardamom pod, star anise, cumin seeds, and cinnamon. Add the drained rice and stir. Cook for 5 minutes on high heat, then drain in a colander.

recipe continues

For Layering

Pinch saffron threads, crushed and steeped in 2 Tbsp boiling water

2 Tbsp ghee

¼ cup chopped fresh coriander (cilantro)

¼ cup chopped fresh mint

To assemble, add the marinated chicken to a large heavy-bottomed pot or Dutch oven and spread into 1 even layer. Sprinkle in the fried onions, and top with the cooked rice. Spread the rice into 1 even layer. Drizzle the soaked saffron threads and their water over the rice, and then drizzle in the ghee. Lastly, sprinkle the fresh coriander and mint on top. Cover the pot with aluminum foil and a lid. Bake for 30 to 35 minutes, then remove from the oven and allow to rest for 5 minutes.

Remove the lid and foil. The rice should look plump and elongated with all the liquid having been absorbed into the grains. Gently fold the rice into the chicken 2 or 3 times. There should be portions of rice that remain white, and portions that have been colored by the chicken and saffron. Leftovers can be stored in an airtight container in the fridge for up to 4 days.

Breads
and
Dosas

Crispy Rava Dosas

MAKES
6 TO 8 DOSAS

½ cup white rice flour

½ cup coarse semolina (rava/sooji)

¼ cup all-purpose flour

1 tsp kosher salt

1 tsp cumin seeds

½ cup finely chopped red onions

¼ cup chopped fresh coriander
  (cilantro)

½ Tbsp finely minced ginger

1 tsp crushed black peppercorns
  (see note)

2 cups water

1 cup buttermilk

3 Tbsp ghee

3 Tbsp canola oil

5-Minute Coconut Chutney
  (page 232), for serving

Simple Sambar (page 63), for serving

If you are looking for a quick way to prepare dosas at home, this is the recipe! Unlike traditional dosas, which require a fermented batter, rava dosa batter requires only 30 minutes of rest time, which is such a win if you're pressed for time. Known for its beautiful lacy appearance and crisp texture, this is personally my favorite type of dosa, and the one I order most when I visit India. Rava dosas are delicious served with 5-Minute Coconut Chutney (page 232) and Simple Sambar (page 63).

To a large bowl, add the rice flour, semolina, all-purpose flour, and salt. Mix until well combined. Add the cumin seeds, red onions, fresh coriander, ginger, and peppercorns, and mix to coat in the flour. Add the water and buttermilk, and whisk to create a thin batter. Allow to rest for 30 minutes.

To a small bowl, add the ghee and oil, and mix to combine.

Heat a large nonstick frying pan on medium-high heat. Dip a folded paper towel lightly into the ghee oil mixture and rub the pan to grease it. Once hot, pour ladlefuls of the rava dosa batter to cover the surface of the pan. The dosa will have several little holes and pockets to contribute to its signature lacy texture.

Let the dosa set for 1½ minutes, then drizzle more of the ghee and oil mixture (1 to 2 Tbsp) around the perimeter and toward the middle of the dosa where the pockets exist. When the dosa is visibly crisp and browned, use a spatula to gently release it from the pan and flip it over. Cook for 1 minute on the other side. Flip again, fold in half, and transfer to a plate. Repeat with the remaining batter.

Serve with coconut chutney and/or sambar.

Note: To get nice pops of heat from the smoky black pepper, I like to gently crush it with a mortar and pestle or with the back of a pan. Unlike the even grind of a pepper mill, this ensures that the peppercorns retain a bit more of their texture, which is ideal for this recipe.

Chili Cheese Parathas

MAKES 8 PARATHAS

For the Dough

1 cup all-purpose whole wheat flour

1 cup all-purpose white flour

1 tsp kosher salt

¼ cup canola oil

¾ cup water (or slightly more)

For the Stuffing

1 cup grated mozzarella cheese

1 cup grated cheddar cheese

½ cup chopped fresh coriander (cilantro)

4 Thai green chilis, thinly sliced

⅓ cup finely chopped red onion

1½ tsp ground cumin

¼ tsp kosher salt

To Finish

¼ cup melted butter

Parathas are flaky flatbreads that can come either plain or stuffed. When stuffed, they are typically filled with a spiced vegetable mixture (like potato, cauliflower, or peas), rolled out, and cooked in a frying pan until toasty on both sides. I could not help but put a twist on this classic by stuffing it with cheese and chilis, a combination typically seen on toast in India. Expect some beautiful cheese pulls with this one!

For the dough, add the whole wheat flour, white flour, and salt to a large bowl. Mix well. Add the oil and mix by hand until sandy in texture. Slowly add the water and mix until a soft dough forms. Form into a ball, place back in the bowl, cover, and allow to rest for 20 minutes at room temperature.

To prepare the stuffing, add the mozzarella cheese, cheddar cheese, fresh coriander, chilis, red onion, cumin, and salt to a medium bowl. Mix to combine.

Divide the dough into 8 equal-sized balls (about the size of a lime).

Place 1 piece of dough on a floured surface, and roll to form a circle at least 4 inches (10 cm) wide. Cover with ⅓ cup of the cheese mixture, leaving a border of dough around the edge. Carefully pull the dough in from the edges toward the middle, and pinch to close.

Flip the stuffed dough over, so that the pinched side is on the bottom. Gently roll with a rolling pin on the lightly floured surface, until about 7 to 8 inches (18 to 20 cm) in diameter. Repeat with the remaining dough and stuffing to make 8 parathas in total.

Place the paratha in a dry pan 1 at a time on high heat, and cook for 2 minutes on each side until golden brown and puffy. Repeat with the remaining parathas.

To finish, brush with melted butter on both sides before serving.

Note: These parathas are a great make-ahead! Roll them out, stack between pieces of parchment paper, then freeze in a resealable plastic bag. To reheat, take a frozen paratha, place it in a frying pan on medium heat, and cook for 3 to 4 minutes on each side until golden brown.

Restaurant-Style Butter Naan

MAKES 5 NAAN

½ cup warm water

½ Tbsp instant yeast

½ Tbsp granulated sugar

3 cups all-purpose white flour

½ Tbsp kosher salt

1 Tbsp plain yogurt

½ cup milk (2% or whole)

¼ cup melted salted butter

Chopped fresh coriander (cilantro),
  for garnish

What is Indian food without naan? It is the first thing I want to order anytime I go out for Indian, and with good reason. While grocery store naan is okay in a pinch, it pales in comparison to this incredible homemade naan, which has a beautiful puffy texture with a slight chew and crispiness. It only takes a handful of ingredients to make the dough, and rolling it out could not be easier once it has rested. Though it is traditionally prepared in a tandoor (a cavernous oven used to cook meat, vegetables, and breads) in restaurants, a super-hot oven works really well at home. Don't forget to be generous with the butter!

To a small bowl, add the water, yeast, and sugar. Stir and allow to sit for 5 minutes. The mixture should become bubbly. If it does not, discard it, purchase new yeast, and start the recipe again.

Add the flour and salt to a large bowl and mix well to combine. Add the bloomed yeast, yogurt, and milk, and mix until a shaggy ball of dough forms. Transfer the dough to the counter and knead until a supple soft ball of dough forms, 5 to 6 minutes.

Place the dough ball back in the bowl, cover with plastic wrap, and allow to rest in a warm place for 1½ hours or until doubled in volume.

Preheat the oven to 500°F.

Divide the dough into 5 equal pieces. Roll each portion into a long oval shape, using a rolling pin and a little extra flour on the counter if necessary.

Place 3 naan on a baking sheet. Bake for 5 to 6 minutes or until the bottom has slightly browned. Flip over and bake for an additional 3 to 4 minutes to brown the other side. Transfer to a platter and tent with foil to keep warm. Repeat this process with the remaining 2 naan.

Brush the baked naan with plenty of melted butter. Garnish with fresh coriander.

Note: To transform butter naan into garlic naan, simply sprinkle ½ Tbsp of chopped garlic over the surface of the rolled dough. Using a rolling pin, roll over the garlic to press it into the dough before baking.

Pull-Apart Curry Leaf Cheese Bread

SERVES 4

½ cup unsalted butter, softened

6 Tbsp curry leaves, divided
  (see note)

1 tsp cumin seeds

1 tsp black peppercorns

½ tsp red chili flakes

3 cloves garlic, finely grated

1 tsp kosher salt

1 crusty loaf of bread
  (French, Italian, or sourdough)

1½ cups grated mozzarella cheese

1 Tbsp canola oil

Mash-up recipes featuring Indian and North American flavors are so fun, which is why I decided to take a classic pull-apart cheese bread and inject it with a little bit of spice! The result is a crusty loaf with hidden pockets of delicious melty cheese and spiced butter. The combination is delectable! Serve this as part of a game day spread with other treats like Nacho Chaat (page 29), Tandoori Fried Chicken Wings with Spicy Lime Honey (page 80), and Cheesy Keema Quesadillas (page 128) as well as a fun drink like Sweet Lime Soda (page 206).

Preheat the oven to 350°F. Line a baking sheet with parchment paper.

To a small blender, add the butter, 3 Tbsp of the curry leaves, cumin seeds, peppercorns, chili flakes, garlic, and salt. Blend until tiny flecks of curry leaves can still be seen.

Transfer the butter to a saucepan and gently warm on medium-low heat for 1 to 2 minutes to toast the spices.

Cut the bread on a diagonal into 1-inch (2.5 cm) diamonds, making sure not to cut through to the bottom. Drizzle melted butter into all the cuts, and stuff them evenly with the cheese. Drizzle the remaining butter over the surface of the bread.

Wrap the bread in aluminum foil and bake for 20 minutes or until the cheese has melted. Uncover and bake for an additional 5 minutes to crisp.

Add the oil to a frying pan on medium-high heat. Once hot, add the remaining 3 Tbsp curry leaves and fry until crisp, about 1 minute. Drain onto a paper towel.

Sprinkle the fried curry leaves over the surface of the bread before serving.

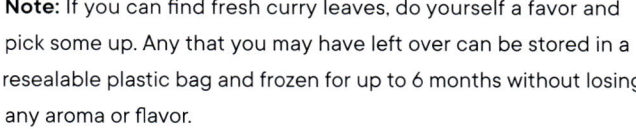

Note: If you can find fresh curry leaves, do yourself a favor and pick some up. Any that you may have left over can be stored in a resealable plastic bag and frozen for up to 6 months without losing any aroma or flavor.

5-Ingredient Chapatis

1 cup all-purpose whole wheat flour

1 cup all-purpose white flour

1 tsp kosher salt

¼ cup canola oil

¾ cup water (or slightly more)

When I think of chapatis, I think of my mom. This was the staple flatbread that she prepared regularly at home, because it was fast, easy, and delicious. The great thing about chapatis is that they contain no leavener and require only 20 minutes of rest time before they're ready to be rolled out. The combination of whole wheat and white flours gives them a beautiful nutty flavor, tender texture, and nice puff. They are perfect with any curry or vegetable side dish, including Express Dhal Makhani (page 53), Paneer Butter Masala (page 60), or Achari Chicken Curry (page 76).

To a bowl, add the whole wheat flour, white flour, and salt. Mix well to combine. Add the oil, and mix until the flour takes on a sandy texture. Gradually pour in the water and mix until a soft dough forms. Form into a ball, and allow to rest in the bowl, covered, for 20 minutes at room temperature.

Lightly flour a work surface. Divide the dough into 8 equal pieces (each about the size of a lime), and roll out into thin circles about 8 inches (20 cm) in diameter.

Heat a frying pan on medium-high heat. Place a rolled dough portion in the pan, and cook until slightly puffed on the first side, 1 minute. Then flip over and cook for an additional 30 to 45 seconds, or until a few brown spots have formed on the other side. Remove from the pan and repeat with the remaining portions of dough.

Enjoy warm.

Puffy Pooris

1 cup all-purpose whole wheat flour

1 cup all-purpose white flour

1 tsp kosher salt

¼ cup canola oil, plus more
  for frying

¾ cup water (or slightly more)

Pooris are the cousin to chapatis, and what you want to prepare if you're looking for a little extra indulgence. The recipes for the dough are the same, with the exception that a poori is deep fried. The result is a big puffy balloon of fried bread that is incredibly impressive! Pooris are delicious served alongside South Indian Potato Masala (page 50) and chickpea curry (30-Minute Amritsari Chole, page 47).

Add the whole wheat flour, white flour, and salt to a large bowl. Whisk to combine. Add the oil and mix until the flour takes on a sandy texture. Gradually pour in the water, mixing continuously until a soft ball of dough forms. Cover and let the dough rest in the bowl for 30 minutes at room temperature.

Lightly flour a work surface. Divide the dough into 8 equal pieces (each about the size of a lime). Roll them out into a thin circle, about 8 inches (20 cm) in diameter.

Pour 3 inches (8 cm) of oil into a deep pot or wok. Heat to 350°F. Gently lower 1 rolled poori into the oil. Using a large slotted spoon, press down on the poori to submerge it into the oil. This will encourage it to puff up. Alternatively, lightly splash the poori with the hot oil.

Cook the poori for 20 to 30 seconds on each side or until lightly golden. Drain on a paper towel. Repeat with the remaining rolled poori.

Serve hot.

Kulchas

MAKES 8 KULCHAS

2 cups all-purpose white flour

½ tsp baking powder

½ tsp baking soda

1 Tbsp sugar

2 tsp salt

2 Tbsp ghee

½ cup lukewarm whole milk

⅓ cup plain yogurt

2 tsp canola oil

Nigella seeds (kalonji), for topping

Chopped fresh coriander (cilantro), for topping

Butter

Kulchas are round leavened flatbreads made with simple pantry ingredients you likely already have on hand. They have a gorgeous chewy texture and a slight crispiness that make them a great pairing for any Indian curry, but especially my chickpea curry (30-Minute Amritsari Chole, page 47). I particularly love the little pops of nigella seeds on top, which not only contribute to the striking presentation, but also offer an oniony bite that is absolutely delicious!

Place the flour, baking powder, baking soda, sugar, and salt in a large bowl. Whisk to combine. Add the ghee and mix by hand until the flour is sandy in texture.

To a large bowl, add the milk and yogurt, and whisk to combine. Add the dry ingredients to the wet ingredients, and stir to form a shaggy wet dough.

Transfer the dough to a lightly floured counter, and knead for 7 to 8 minutes until a smooth, supple ball of dough forms. Coat with the oil and cover with a damp cloth. Rest for 1 hour.

Divide the dough into 8 equal pieces (each about the size of a lime). Dust lightly with flour and roll them out into 8-inch (20 cm) circles. Sprinkle the nigella seeds and coriander overtop, and use a rolling pin to press them into the dough. Flip the dough over and wet the bottom with a little bit of water.

Heat a frying pan on medium-high heat on a gas stove. Once hot, place 1 rolled dough disk, wet side down, into the pan. Allow the kulcha to bubble up and puff for 1 to 1½ minutes. Then flip the pan over and hover over the flame, moving the pan so that it evenly browns the surface. Repeat with the remaining disks. Alternatively, bake 1 to 2 kulchas on a pizza stone in a 500°F oven for 5 to 6 minutes until bubbly and slightly crisp. Repeat with the remaining disks.

Gently pry from the pan and rub butter all over the top.

4-Ingredient Dosas
Rice and Lentil Crêpes

3 cups basmati rice

1 cup skinless urad dhal (black gram)

1 tsp fenugreek seeds

2 tsp kosher salt

¼ cup melted ghee

South Indian Potato Masala
  (page 50), for serving (optional)

Simple Sambar (page 63), for serving

5-Ingredient Coconut Chutney
  (page 232), for serving

Whenever I describe dosas to someone who has never had them before, I explain that they're the Indian equivalent of crêpes, which gives people a sense of what they look like. But when we're talking preparation, flavor, and texture, dosas are a completely different ball game. Prepared with a fermented batter made of rice and lentils (perfect for those who don't eat gluten!), the batter is spread out on a hot frying pan, and then drizzled with ghee to help a crisp and golden surface form. It can be served with a savory accompaniment or even as a sweet with a combination of ghee and sugar, or even chocolate hazelnut spread.

Add the rice, urad dhal, and fenugreek seeds to a bowl. Cover with warm water and massage the rice and dhal until the water turns cloudy. Drain and repeat until the water runs clear. Soak for 4 hours.

Place the soaked grains in a blender and pour in enough cold water to just barely cover the grains (about 3 cups). Blend, adding more water if necessary, to create a thick, smooth batter that is pourable (similar to the consistency of pancake batter). Add the salt and quickly blend to incorporate.

Pour the batter into a bowl and cover loosely with a cloth. Place in a warm area for 8 to 10 hours to ferment. The batter will expand to about 3 times its volume and become puffy in texture with a distinct sour aroma.

Heat a large nonstick frying pan on medium heat. Once hot, dip a paper towel lightly into the ghee and rub the surface of the pan.

Pour ⅓ cup of the fermented batter into the center of the pan with a measuring cup. Using the flat bottom of the measuring cup, begin pushing out the batter from the center of the pan in a circular motion to create a thin crêpe.

Drizzle 1 Tbsp of ghee around the edges and toward the middle of the dosa. Cook for 1 minute or until golden brown and crispy, then flip and cook the other side for 20 to 30 seconds to set.

Fill with the potato masala, if desired, and fold in half. Serve warm with sambar and coconut chutney.

Besan ka Cheela
Vegetarian Omelets

1 cup chickpea flour

¼ cup finely chopped red onion

¼ cup finely chopped seeded tomato

2 Thai green chilis, thinly sliced

1 tsp finely grated ginger

3 Tbsp chopped fresh coriander (cilantro)

¼ tsp cayenne chili powder

¼ tsp ground turmeric

½ tsp carom seeds (ajwain)

½ tsp kosher salt

⅔ cup water

Canola oil, for frying

Chickpea flour is very popular in Indian cuisine in both sweet and savory recipes, and especially vegetarian dishes. Its distinct nutty flavor works really well in a recipe like this when paired with bright and fresh aromatics. It also happens to be gluten-free, which makes it an excellent option for those who can't eat gluten. Besan ka cheela is a hearty pancake flavored with onions, chilis, ginger, and spices. It has a beautiful yellow color, which is why it's often called a vegetarian omelet, a great substitute for those who don't eat eggs. Serve it for breakfast or brunch with a cup of Masala Chai on the side (page 212).

To a large bowl, add the chickpea flour, onion, tomato, chilis, ginger, fresh coriander, chili powder, turmeric, carom seeds, and salt. Mix to coat the vegetables with the flour.

Slowly pour in the water, stirring until a loose batter forms.

Heat a large nonstick frying pan on medium-low heat and slightly grease with oil. Add ⅓ to ½ cup of the batter to the center of the pan, and spread it with a ladle, moving in a circular motion to form a round pancake. Drizzle 2 tsp of oil around the edges of the pancake. Cook until the bottom has browned and the top has set. Flip over and cook until the other side becomes slightly golden. Repeat with the remaining batter.

Remove from the pan and serve.

Sweets

Tapioca Payasam

SERVES 6

5 cups water

½ cup mini tapioca/sago pearls

5 cups whole milk

¾ cup condensed milk

¼ cup white sugar

1½ tsp ground cardamom

Pinch saffron threads

¼ cup ghee

¼ cup whole cashews

¼ cup slivered almonds

When I think of desserts that are most frequently served after an Indian meal, payasam is the first one that comes to mind. A creamy pudding often flavored with cardamom and saffron, this version features tapioca pearls, which can easily be found at Asian grocery stores. I love the beautiful soft and springy texture that they bring to this classic dessert.

Add the water to a medium saucepan and bring to a boil. Add the tapioca and stir. Reduce the heat to low and cook for 20 minutes, stirring occasionally, until the tapioca is translucent. Drain in a mesh sieve, and rinse with cold water until the tapioca is no longer hot. Transfer to a bowl.

Add the whole milk to a medium pot, and heat on medium-high. Cook, stirring frequently, for 10 minutes, or until slightly reduced. Stir in the condensed milk and sugar and continue cooking for 5 minutes, stirring frequently.

Sprinkle in the cardamom and crush the saffron threads between your fingers, then add to the milk as well. Stir the spices into the milk and simmer for a minute, then remove from the heat.

Heat the ghee in a small frying pan on medium heat. Once hot, add the cashews and fry for 3 to 4 minutes or until golden brown. Remove with a slotted spoon and drain onto a paper towel.

Add the cooked tapioca to the milk mixture along with the fried cashews and almonds. Stir to combine.

Serve warm, or chill for 3 hours before serving in glasses or small bowls.

5-Ingredient Saffron Pistachio Kulfi

SERVES 8 TO 10

2 cups + 2 Tbsp cold whipping (35%) cream, divided

Pinch saffron threads

½ cup shelled unsalted pistachios

14 oz sweetened condensed milk

½ tsp ground cardamom

⅛ tsp kosher salt

India's answer to ice cream, kulfi is a firm-set frozen treat that is traditionally made with milk that has been boiled down until creamy and then flavored with spices, nuts, and/or fruit. To simplify this process, I like making kulfi with a base of whipped cream and condensed milk, which deliver both richness and deep milky flavor. The saffron and cardamom add a beautiful fragrance to this dessert and are further complemented by the nutty, buttery pistachios.

Heat 2 Tbsp of the cream (in the microwave or on the stove) until very hot. Crush the saffron threads between your fingers into the cream. Stir and allow to steep for 5 minutes.

Add the pistachios to a food processor and pulse until almost finely ground with a few coarse pieces.

Pour the condensed milk into a medium bowl and add the steeped saffron cream, ground pistachios, cardamom, and salt. Whisk to combine.

Whisk the remaining 2 cups of cream in a large bowl until stiff peaks form. Pour the condensed milk mixture into the cream, and gently fold until incorporated.

Spoon the mixture into silicone popsicle molds, top with their sticks, and freeze for a minimum of 6 hours.

Gently unmold and serve. These kulfis can be stored in the freezer for up to 4 months.

Easy Rasmalai Ice Cream

SERVES 6

2 cups + 2 Tbsp cold whipping (35%) cream, divided

Pinch saffron threads

14 oz sweetened condensed milk

1 cup full-fat ricotta

1 tsp ground cardamom

½ cup slivered almonds, divided, plus more for serving

½ cup crushed pistachios, divided, plus more for serving

Pomegranate seeds, for serving

6 vanilla pizzelle wafer cookies, for serving

Rasmalai is an Indian dessert of fresh pressed cheese steeped in a sweet spiced milk. The entire process of making rasmalai can take over a day, which is why I wanted to find a shortcut to achieve the same flavors but in a different way. Enter rasmalai ice cream! Creamy, dreamy, and oh so good, this recipe features store-bought ricotta, which provides the same flavor profile and texture offered by a classic rasmalai.

Heat 2 Tbsp of the cream (in the microwave or on the stove) until very hot. Crush the saffron threads between your fingers into the cream. Stir and allow to steep for 5 minutes.

Add the remaining 2 cups of cream to a large bowl and whisk until stiff peaks form.

To a medium bowl, add the condensed milk, ricotta, steeped saffron cream, and cardamom and mix until well combined. Pour the ricotta mixture into the whipped cream, and gently fold together.

Pour half of the mixture into a 5 × 9-inch (13 × 23 cm) loaf tin and sprinkle ¼ cup of the almonds and ¼ cup of the pistachios evenly over the surface. Pour the remaining cream mixture overtop, smoothing it into an even layer, and top with the remaining ¼ cup almonds and ¼ cup pistachios.

Cover with plastic wrap and aluminum foil, and freeze for 4 to 6 hours, or until frozen. Remove from the freezer 15 minutes before serving to allow it to soften slightly.

To serve, scoop the ice cream into bowls and garnish with slivered almonds, crushed pistachios, pomegranate seeds, and a pizzelle wafer cookie.

Classic Gulab Jamun

SERVES 8

½ cup whole milk

4 Tbsp ghee

1½ cups milk powder

3 cups sugar

1 cup water

Pinch saffron threads

½ tsp rose water

¼ cup all-purpose white flour

¾ tsp baking powder

¼ tsp kosher salt

Canola oil, for deep frying

Crushed pistachios, for garnish

Dried rose petals (optional),
  for garnish

Gulab jamun is one of the most popular Indian desserts of all time. Custardy round fritters soaked in a saffron syrup until plump and juicy . . . this sweet is absolutely irresistible! The key to victory with this recipe is to take your time frying the gulab jamun, and make sure it has enough time to soak so that it can double or even triple in volume. If you're feeling extra indulgent, serve it à la mode with some cold vanilla or pistachio ice cream.

To a medium nonstick pan, add the whole milk, ghee, and milk powder. Mix well to combine. Heat on medium, and cook for 5 minutes, stirring continuously, until a thick paste forms. The paste should pull away from the sides of the pan. Transfer to a bowl and cool completely.

Add the sugar and water to a medium pot. Bring to a simmer and cook for 5 minutes or until the sugar has completely dissolved. Crush in the saffron threads, add the rose water, and stir. Cover to keep warm.

Add the flour, baking powder, and salt to a small bowl. Whisk to combine, then add this mixture to the cooled milk paste, and mix until well incorporated.

Divide the dough into 16 pieces about the size of a ping-pong ball. Roll each piece of dough between your palms to create a round ball.

Add 3 inches (8 cm) of oil to a deep pot or wok, and heat on medium-low. Once the oil reaches 300°F, add 8 dough balls and gently stir, keeping the dough balls in motion for 10 minutes, or until the gulab jamun have doubled in size and are a deep golden brown.

Remove the fried dough balls with a slotted spoon and immediately add to the pot containing the warm syrup, stirring and pushing the balls into the syrup to help with absorption. Fry the remaining dough balls and add them to the pot as well.

Let the gulab jamun soak for a minimum of 1½ hours before serving. To serve, garnish with the pistachios and rose petals, if desired.

Mango Lassi Cake

For the Cake

½ cup unsalted butter,
   at room temperature

½ cup canola oil

1½ cups granulated sugar

4 large eggs

2 tsp ground cardamom

Pinch saffron threads, crushed

3 cups all-purpose white flour

1 Tbsp baking powder

¾ tsp kosher salt

1¼ cups buttermilk

For the Mango Syrup

¼ cup sugar

¼ cup water

¼ cup tinned kesar or alphonso
   mango pulp

For the Mango Cream

3 cups cold whipping (35%) cream

3 Tbsp icing sugar

¾ cup kesar or alphonso mango pulp

For Assembly

1½ cups peeled and chopped
   ripe mango

⅓ cup chopped pistachios

If you have something to celebrate, big or small, this is the cake to do it with! Featuring the flavors of the oh-so-loved Indian drink mango lassi, this layered cake features a sponge scented with cardamom and saffron, mango whipped cream, and lots of fresh, sweet mango. Lightly sweet with beautiful tropical notes, this will be the star at any dessert table.

To prepare the cake, preheat the oven to 350°F. Grease and line two 9-inch (23 cm) round cake pans with butter and parchment paper.

Cream together the butter, oil, and sugar using a stand mixer or with an electric hand mixer in a large bowl, until light and creamy. Add 1 egg and mix until incorporated. Repeat 1 by 1 with the remaining eggs. Add the cardamom and saffron, and mix to combine.

To a separate bowl, add the flour, baking powder, and salt. Whisk together.

Add one-quarter of the dry ingredients to the butter mixture, and gently mix on the lowest setting of a stand mixer or with an electric mixer. Add one-quarter of the buttermilk, and mix again. Repeat the process for the remaining dry ingredients and buttermilk until just incorporated.

Divide the batter evenly between the 2 prepared cake pans and bake for 25 minutes or until a toothpick inserted in the middle comes out clean. Allow the cakes to cool in their tins for 10 minutes before inverting onto a wire rack to cool completely.

To prepare the mango syrup, add the sugar, water, and mango pulp to a small saucepan. Bring to a simmer and cook for 5 minutes or until the sugar has dissolved. Allow to cool completely.

Brush a thin layer of the cooled syrup over the tops of the cake rounds and let it soak for 5 to 10 minutes. Repeat 1 more time.

To prepare the mango cream, whisk the cream with the icing sugar in a large bowl until stiff peaks form. Fold in the mango pulp until just incorporated.

recipe continues

To assemble, top 1 cake layer with half of the mango cream and spread to cover. Scatter half the chopped mango and half the crushed pistachios overtop.

Add the second cake layer on top (syrup side facing the cream). Top with the remaining mango cream, chopped mango, and crushed pistachios.

Cut into slices and serve. Store leftovers in an airtight container in the fridge for up to 3 days.

Cardamom Orange Tiramisu

SERVES 4

3 Darjeeling tea bags

1½ cups boiling water

3 large eggs, separated into yolks
   and whites

½ cup granulated sugar

⅓ cup finely ground pistachios

Zest of 1 orange, plus more
   for garnish

½ tsp ground cardamom

1 cup mascarpone

12 ladyfinger biscuits

1 cup orange segments

Cocoa powder, for dusting

Slivered pistachios, for garnish

Tiramisu is a delicious make-ahead dessert, and is quick to prepare, which makes it the perfect treat for parties and special occasions. Instead of dipping the ladyfinger biscuits in espresso, I take a detour with beloved Darjeeling tea, which gives the tiramisu a delicate citrusy flavor. Combined with the floral cardamom, buttery pistachios, and sweet orange segments, this tiramisu veers far from the classic but is incredibly tasty!

Place the tea bags in the boiling water and steep for 5 minutes. Remove the tea bags and allow the tea to cool.

Whisk the egg whites in a stand mixer, or with an electric whisk in a large bowl, until stiff peaks form.

To a medium bowl, add the sugar and egg yolks and whisk until pale, fluffy, and voluminous. Whisk in the ground pistachios, orange zest, and cardamom. Add the mascarpone and whisk until incorporated. Add a quarter of the egg whites to the mascarpone mixture and gently fold to incorporate. Continue adding, a quarter at a time, and gently folding. The resulting mixture should be voluminous, light, and fluffy.

Split the biscuits in half. Dip 2 of the biscuit halves quickly in the cooled tea, and layer at the bottom of a whiskey glass. Top with a generous dollop of cardamom orange cream and arrange a couple of orange segments on top so that they cover the surface of the cream.

Quickly dip 2 more pieces of biscuit and layer on top, followed by more cardamom orange cream. Repeat this process 1 more time and fill the glass with the cardamom orange cream, heaping the cream to overfill the glass. Using a bench scraper or pastry knife, scrape off the excess cream so that a clean, smooth top forms.

Dust with cocoa until completely covered and garnish with slivered pistachios and some freshly grated orange zest. Repeat the process with the remaining ingredients to make 4 tiramisu cups in all.

Refrigerate for a minimum of 3 to 4 hours to let the cookies soften before serving.

Malpuas

SERVES 6

1 cup all-purpose white flour

½ tsp baking powder

½ tsp ground cardamom

½ tsp ground fennel seed

½ tsp kosher salt

½ cup sweetened condensed milk

⅔ cup whole milk

1 cup granulated sugar

½ cup water

Pinch saffron threads, plus more for garnish

Canola oil, for deep frying

¼ cup coarsely chopped pistachios

Malpuas are fluffy deep-fried pancakes soaked in syrup. They are typically served during festivals like Holi and Diwali, and are flavored with floral cardamom and fennel. Crispy on the outside, with a slight chew in the middle, you might get tempted to stack these high for breakfast, and I don't blame you.

To a large bowl, add the flour, baking powder, cardamom, fennel seed, and salt. Whisk to combine. Pour in the condensed milk and whole milk and whisk until a thick batter forms.

To a medium saucepan, add the sugar and water. Bring to a simmer, stir, and cook for 5 minutes or until all the sugar has dissolved. Continue cooking for 3 to 4 minutes or until the syrup thickens slightly. Remove from the heat and crush in the saffron threads. Cover to keep warm.

Add 1 inch (2.5 cm) of oil to a large frying pan over medium heat. When the oil is about 350°F, gently pour ¼ cup of the batter into the pan to form the malpua. Cook for 1½ minutes on each side or until golden and crispy on the outside, and fluffy and cooked through the middle. Repeat with the remaining batter.

Place the warm malpuas directly into the saffron syrup for 30 seconds, flipping to coat.

Transfer to a serving dish and garnish with pistachios and saffron threads. Serve warm.

Jaggery Apple Blossoms

MAKES 6
APPLE BLOSSOMS

6 cups peeled and chopped apples
  (I like Honeycrisp or Granny Smith)
½ cup powdered jaggery
¼ cup granulated sugar
2 tsp ground cardamom
1 tsp ground ginger
1 package (1 lb/454 g) thawed
  phyllo dough
1 cup melted salted butter
Vanilla ice cream, for serving

Jaggery is a type of unrefined cane sugar used in India for sweets and occasionally savory preparations. It is rich in flavor with notes of molasses and deep caramel, and is often paired with dry spices in desserts. In this recipe, jaggery replaces brown sugar for a fresh take on apple pie. Store-bought phyllo is a great shortcut in this recipe, as it results in a super-crisp pastry without the hassle of making the dough from scratch.

Preheat the oven to 425°F. Line 2 baking sheets with parchment paper, and arrange 2 oven racks toward the middle of the oven.

Add the apples, jaggery, granulated sugar, cardamom, and ginger to a large bowl. Mix to combine.

Layer 3 pieces of phyllo dough, brushing the melted butter between each layer. Place 1 cup of the apple mixture in the center of the dough, and pull the pastry up toward the middle, pinching to close.

Repeat the process with the remaining phyllo and apple mixture, making 6 apple blossoms in total.

Place 3 apple blossoms on each prepared baking sheet and place each tray on a separate rack in the oven. Bake for 20 minutes, rotating the trays from the upper to lower position and vice versa halfway through baking, until the phyllo is crispy and golden brown.

Transfer to a plate and serve hot, warm, or at room temperature with vanilla ice cream.

20-Minute Badam Halwa

SERVES 6

1 cup almond flour

¾ cup whole milk

4 Tbsp ghee, divided

½ cup granulated sugar

¼ tsp yellow food coloring

1 tsp ground cardamom

Pinch saffron threads

¼ cup slivered almonds

Badam halwa is one of the easiest Indian desserts to prepare as it features common pantry ingredients and a quick prep time (20 minutes!). Celebrating almonds (badam), its texture can be compared to a soft-set fudge flavored with nutty ghee, cardamom, and saffron. This is a rich dessert, so I like serving it in small bowls, though that hasn't prevented many family members and friends from coming back for seconds and thirds.

Add the almond flour and milk to a blender. Blend until thickened but still slightly coarse in texture.

Add the almond paste to a medium nonstick pot, followed by 2 Tbsp of the ghee, sugar, and yellow food coloring. Heat the mixture on medium heat and stir constantly for 8 minutes until the mixture slightly thickens. Add the cardamom and saffron and continue stirring for another 8 minutes or until the halwa doesn't stick to the sides of the pan. Stir in the remaining 2 Tbsp of ghee.

Pour the halwa into a bowl. Garnish with slivered almonds. Serve hot, warm, or at room temperature.

Store in an airtight container in the fridge for up to 2 weeks. To reheat, warm in the microwave.

Pineapple Kesari

SERVES 6

2 cups chopped pineapple

2 cups granulated sugar, divided

½ cup ghee, divided

½ cup raw cashews

1 cup coarse semolina

3 cups water

¼ tsp yellow food coloring

1 tsp ground cardamom

Pinch saffron threads

How do you make an iconic Indian dessert even more delicious? With the addition of candied pineapple. I don't know how or when my mom came up with this idea, but the incorporation of fruity tropical pineapple to kesari, a rich semolina pudding, was an absolute game changer. It tops the list as one of the most requested desserts on her catering menu, and rightfully so!

To a medium saucepan, add the chopped pineapple and ½ cup of the sugar. Bring to a simmer and cook for 10 to 12 minutes or until a thick syrup forms.

Add ¼ cup of the ghee to a medium nonstick pot on medium heat. Add the cashews and fry until lightly golden. Remove the cashews with a slotted spoon and reserve in a bowl.

Add the semolina to the same pot, and toast for 1½ to 2 minutes, stirring constantly, until lightly golden and nutty in aroma (do not brown). Transfer to a bowl.

Add the water to the pot along with the yellow food coloring and bring to a simmer. Slowly pour the toasted semolina into the water, whisking continuously so that no lumps form. Turn off the heat, then stir in the remaining 1½ cups of sugar, ¼ cup ghee, cardamom, saffron, and candied pineapple.

Increase the heat to medium and cook the kesari, stirring constantly, for 5 minutes to cook the semolina. Remove from the heat and stir in the fried cashews.

Serve warm or at room temperature.

Drinks

Mango Lassi

SERVES 2

1 cup frozen mango chunks

½ cup tinned mango pulp (see note)

⅓ cup plain yogurt

1 cup whole milk

1 Tbsp white sugar

¼ tsp ground cardamom

¼ cup diced ripe mango

2 Tbsp crushed pistachios

Icy cold, refreshing, and fruity, there is no missing mango lassi when you look at an Indian restaurant menu. It is the quintessential drink to accompany any Indian meal, as the yogurt and milk help tame the heat, should things get a bit spicy. Also, its super tropical and slightly floral flavor makes it a favorite with kids and adults alike. My version uses frozen mango as the base, which helps chill the drink and gives it a beautiful velvety texture. Simply throw all the ingredients in a blender and blend away. It's so easy!

To a blender, add the frozen mango, mango pulp, yogurt, milk, sugar, and cardamom. Blend until smooth and pour into a tall glass.

Garnish with the diced mango and crushed pistachios.

Note: Tinned mango pulp is a processed mango product containing puréed kesar or alphonso mangoes sweetened with sugar. It can be found in the international aisle of some grocery stores, and most often at Indian grocery stores. It has a deep aromatic mango flavor that makes this lassi extra special.

Sweet Lime Soda

For the Simple Syrup
½ cup granulated sugar
½ cup water

For Assembly
Juice of 2 limes
1½ cups cold club soda
Thinly sliced rounds of lime

This is the most refreshing drink, and it's the one I reach for often on blistering summer days. While I use simple syrup in this recipe to sweeten the drink, sometimes I also add a pinch or two of salt for a more sweet and savory vibe. So good!

To make the simple syrup, in a small saucepan, add the sugar and water. Bring to a simmer and cook for 2 minutes or until the sugar has dissolved. Allow to cool.

To assemble, add ¼ cup of the simple syrup (or more/less to taste) to a tall glass. Add the lime juice and stir to mix. Top with the club soda and stir again.

Garnish with a few slices of lime in the glass.

Paneer Soda

Rose Soda

For the Rose Syrup
½ cup granulated sugar
½ cup water
½ tsp rose water

For Assembly
1½ cups cold club soda

Roses are a highly revered flower in India and are used in many different ways, including decor, ayurveda, perfumes, and even food and drink. In this soda, the rose provides a delicate floral aroma and aids with cooling the body. It's the ideal drink to have on a hot summer day when you're looking for a bit of relief from the heat.

To make the rose syrup, in a small saucepan, add the sugar and water. Bring to a simmer and cook for 2 minutes or until the sugar has dissolved. Allow to cool, then stir in the rose water.

To assemble, fill a glass one-quarter of the way with the rose syrup. Top with the club soda and stir to mix.

Coconut Shake

SERVES 2

1 cup young coconut flesh
  (see note)

1 cup coconut water

½ cup whole milk

3 Tbsp granulated sugar

1 cup ice

No trip to India is complete without a few stops along the road for fresh coconut water. But sometimes when I'm craving something a little more indulgent, I make this coconut shake. The tiny chunks of blended coconut flesh really make it extra special!

Add the coconut flesh, coconut water, milk, sugar, and ice to a blender. Blend until smooth and thick.

Pour into 2 glasses and serve with a straw.

Note: Young coconut can be obtained from cutting a young coconut in half and scooping out the flesh. Alternatively, it can also be found in the freezer section of most Asian grocery stores. If you can't find young coconut, use the same amount of fresh or frozen coconut chunks.

Masala Chai

1 cinnamon stick

1 star anise

4 cloves

4 green cardamom pods

½ tsp black peppercorns

½ Tbsp freshly grated ginger

3 cups water

4 Tbsp black tea leaves (Darjeeling
if available) or 3 black tea bags

2 cups whole milk

Granulated sugar

Masala chai is the epitome of comfort in a cup. I like crushing whole spices for this recipe, as they maximize the aroma and flavor of the tea. While tea is often associated with breakfast time, masala chai is drunk all through the day in India as an instant pick-me-up. Served with breakfast dishes like 5-Ingredient Masala Omelet (page 71) or snacks like Crispy Onion and Jalapeño Pakodas (page 26), you can't go wrong with a large cup of chai on the side.

Place the cinnamon, star anise, cloves, cardamom pods, and peppercorns in a small resealable plastic bag. Seal the bag and crush the spices lightly with a rolling pin or a heavy-bottomed saucepan.

Add the water to a medium saucepan and bring to a simmer. Add the crushed spices and freshly grated ginger and simmer for 3 minutes. Remove from the heat and add the black tea leaves (or tea bags). Steep for 10 minutes.

Strain the tea into another pot, discarding the crushed spices and tea. Add the milk and bring the tea back up to a bare simmer to warm through.

Pour into teacups and stir in sugar to taste.

Badam Milk

SERVES 4

¾ cup blanched whole almonds
 (skin off)

4 cups whole milk, divided

½ tsp ground cardamom

Pinch saffron threads

⅓ cup granulated sugar

¼ cup slivered almonds

2 Tbsp crushed pistachios

Growing up, my mom would always have a batch of cold badam (almond) milk waiting for us in the fridge when we got back from school. My brother and I would drink multiple cupfuls with delight, enjoying the creamy but slightly gritty texture, the crunch of the nuts, and the aroma of cardamom and saffron. Think of it like a milkshake, but Indian-style! I also like to serve it for dessert, as it is a light and refreshing way to end an Indian meal.

Place the almonds in a bowl and cover with hot water. Soak for 30 minutes to soften, then drain.

Add the almonds to a small blender along with 1 cup of milk. Blend until smooth.

Add the remaining milk to a saucepan and bring to a simmer. Add the cardamom and crush the saffron threads into the pan. Cook for 6 to 7 minutes on medium heat, stirring often, until slightly reduced.

Whisk in the ground almond paste, and simmer for 2 minutes. Add the sugar and stir to dissolve. Remove from the heat and add the slivered almonds.

Serve hot or cold. Garnish with crushed pistachios before serving.

Rose Milk

For the Rose Syrup

½ cup granulated sugar

½ cup water

¼ tsp rose essence
  (or ¾ tsp rose water)

¼ tsp pink food coloring

For Assembly

2 cups cold milk

1 cup ice

I could spot a glass of rose milk from a mile away just from its magnificent color. An icy drink of milk flavored with rose, this beverage is consumed widely around India and is also used as the base for the popular ice cream float, falooda. Rose milk is popular during the hot summer months in India for its ability to quickly cool down the body. Feature it at your next barbecue, or bring it chilled in a thermos to your picnic for a fun treat.

To make the rose syrup, add the sugar and water to a saucepan. Bring to a simmer and cook for 5 to 6 minutes or until the sugar has dissolved and the syrup has thickened slightly. Remove from the heat and stir in the rose essence and pink food coloring. Transfer to a jar and allow to cool completely.

To assemble, add the cold milk to a blender and ¼ cup (or more to taste) of the rose syrup. Blend until frothy.

Divide the ice between 2 glasses and top with the rose milk.

Neer Mor
Spiced Buttermilk

SERVES 4

1 cup plain yogurt

4 cups cold water

2 tsp ground cumin

Kosher salt

2 Thai green chilis, finely minced

2-inch (5 cm) knob ginger, finely grated

½ cup peeled and shredded green mango (see note)

1 Tbsp canola oil

1 tsp black mustard seeds

2 Tbsp curry leaves

Many Indian drinks are prepared with the purpose of cooling down the body. My mom would make spiced buttermilk when we would go for picnics where we would be out in the sun for hours. While traditionally made with buttermilk (the liquid left behind after churning butter), she would use yogurt to bring a similar creamy tang without all the work. The cooling nature of the yogurt would help quench our thirst, while the fiery green chilis and crunchy mango would perk up our taste buds. If you haven't had a savory beverage before, this is a great place to start.

Add the yogurt, water, and cumin to a blender. Season with salt to taste and blend until frothy.

Transfer to a bowl and add the chilis. Take the ginger and squeeze it between your fingers to release just the juice into the mixture, discarding the fibers. Add the green mango and mix.

Add the oil to a small frying pan and heat on medium-high. Once hot, add the black mustard seeds and let them crackle for 10 to 15 seconds. Tear up the curry leaves, add them to the oil, and mix for 5 to 10 seconds. Pour the hot spiced oil into the mixture and stir well.

Chill in a pitcher in the fridge for 1 hour. Divide between 4 glasses.

Note: To shred the green mango, julienne using a mandoline or food processor, or finely chop by hand.

South Indian Filter Coffee

SERVES 2

3 Tbsp ground coffee with chicory
½ cup boiling water
1 cup whole milk
Granulated sugar

Though I am not a coffee drinker, I can never say no to a cup of traditional filter coffee. Frothy, creamy, and rich, this coffee is a staple at breakfast and around tiffin time (4 p.m.) in India. If you are keen on preparing this coffee regularly, I do recommend investing in a simple filter coffee maker; however, I've also included a quick hack using things you can find in your kitchen.

Place the coffee in the perforated top compartment of a South Indian filter coffee maker. Press down gently to compact the coffee grounds. Pour the boiling water overtop, cover, and allow the coffee to drip down to the bottom compartment for 20 minutes.

Alternatively, line a small wire mesh sieve with cheesecloth, and rest it on top of a small bowl. Place the ground coffee in a mound in the middle of the cheesecloth and push down with the back of a spoon to compact. Pour the boiling water overtop and let the coffee drip down into the bowl for 20 minutes.

Add the milk to a small saucepan and bring to a boil. Reduce the heat, and simmer for 5 minutes to slightly reduce.

Pour 1 to 1½ Tbsp of the drip coffee into the bottom of a small glass. Add sugar to taste, and top with ½ cup of the hot milk. Pour the drink into another glass of similar size. Pour the coffee back and forth a few times to help blend the sugar and aerate the coffee so that it's nice and frothy. (This process can also be done using a traditional South Indian coffee dabra set.)

Tamarind Soda

SERVES 4

Tamarind Syrup

½ cup water

½ cup granulated sugar

3 Tbsp tamarind paste

1 tsp kosher salt

For Assembly

1 cup ice, divided

Crushed cumin seeds

Mint leaves

Cold club soda

This soda highlights the flavor of tangy and fruity tamarind. Tamarind can be found fresh in pods, as a paste sold in blocks, and in concentrate form. I suggest the paste for this recipe, as it is the easiest to work with and yields the best flavor.

To make the tamarind syrup, add the water, granulated sugar, tamarind paste, and salt to a saucepan. Bring to a simmer, whisking to incorporate the tamarind paste and dissolve the sugar. Cook for 2 minutes, or until slightly thickened. Strain over a fine mesh sieve into a glass jar and allow to cool completely.

To assemble, fill a glass a quarter of the way up with the cooled syrup. Add ¼ cup of the ice, a pinch of crushed cumin, and a few mint leaves. Slowly pour in the club soda, mixing continuously.

Sauces, Spice Blends, Condiments, and Fresh Things

Wedding Mango Pickle

MAKES 2 CUPS

2 cups finely diced green mango (see note)

1 Tbsp cayenne chili powder

1 tsp ground turmeric

1 Tbsp kosher salt

3 Tbsp white vinegar

2 Tbsp canola oil

2 tsp black mustard seeds

¼ tsp asafoetida

One of the things I most look forward to at an Indian wedding is the lunch served right after. A variety of vegetarian dishes are laid out on a banana leaf, but the one I always seek out first is the mango pickle: finely chopped tart green mango marinated with chili, vinegar, and spices. It's the condiment that gets my taste buds excited for the rest of the meal. This pickle is the perfect accompaniment for curd rice (see Thayir Sadam, page 141) and a staple condiment to have on the table for any Indian meal, as it brings a bit of heat and acidity to the mix.

Place the mango, chili powder, turmeric, salt, and vinegar in a bowl. Mix to combine.

Heat the oil in a small frying pan on medium-high heat. Once hot, add the mustard seeds and let them crackle for 10 to 15 seconds, then add the asafoetida.

Pour the hot oil over the spiced mangoes and mix to combine.

Serve immediately, or store in a glass jar and refrigerate for up to 2 weeks.

Note: Green mangoes typically have a fine thin green skin with white crunchy flesh on the inside that is tart. This type of mango can be found at Asian grocery stores. There is no need to peel green mangoes. If you're having a hard time finding green mango, an unripe Mexican mango (apple mango) can be substituted so long as it is rock hard to the touch. Just be sure to peel it, as the skin of Mexican mangoes is much thicker.

Kachumber Salad

SERVES 4

1 medium tomato, seeded
  and chopped

½ cucumber, seeded and chopped

1 small sweet white onion, chopped

¼ cup pomegranate seeds

2 Thai green chilis, thinly sliced

¼ cup chopped fresh coriander
  (cilantro)

Juice of 1 lemon

Kosher salt

It's always nice to have a salad to contribute an element of freshness to Indian meals. I love the pops of pomegranate in this one, as they add unexpected bursts of sweetness that work really well with the crunchy veggies and fiery chilis. Kachumber salad is a great side to have on the table and is perfect paired with curries like Classic Chicken Tikka Masala (page 89), Lamb Rogan Josh (page 132), and Baingan ka Bharta (page 67).

Add the tomato, cucumber, onion, pomegranate seeds, and chilis to a medium bowl. Season with the lemon juice and salt to taste. Mix to combine.

Cucumber Pomegranate Raita

MAKES 4 CUPS

2 cups plain yogurt

1 English cucumber, peeled,
  seeded, and finely diced

½ cup pomegranate seeds

1 tsp ground cumin

3 Tbsp thinly sliced mint leaves

¼ cup chopped fresh coriander
  (cilantro)

Kosher salt

When things get a bit too spicy, raita is always there to the rescue! This cool yogurt sauce is great at tempering the heat of Indian meals. I always have raita on the table when I'm serving dishes like chickpea curry (30-Minute Amritsari Chole, page 47), Hyderabadi Chicken Biryani (page 155), and Lamb Karahi (page 121). It is also great served as a dip with chips or toasted pita triangles as an appetizer.

To a bowl, add the yogurt, cucumber, pomegranate seeds, cumin, mint, and fresh coriander. Season with salt to taste and mix to combine.

Store in an airtight container in the fridge for up to 3 days.

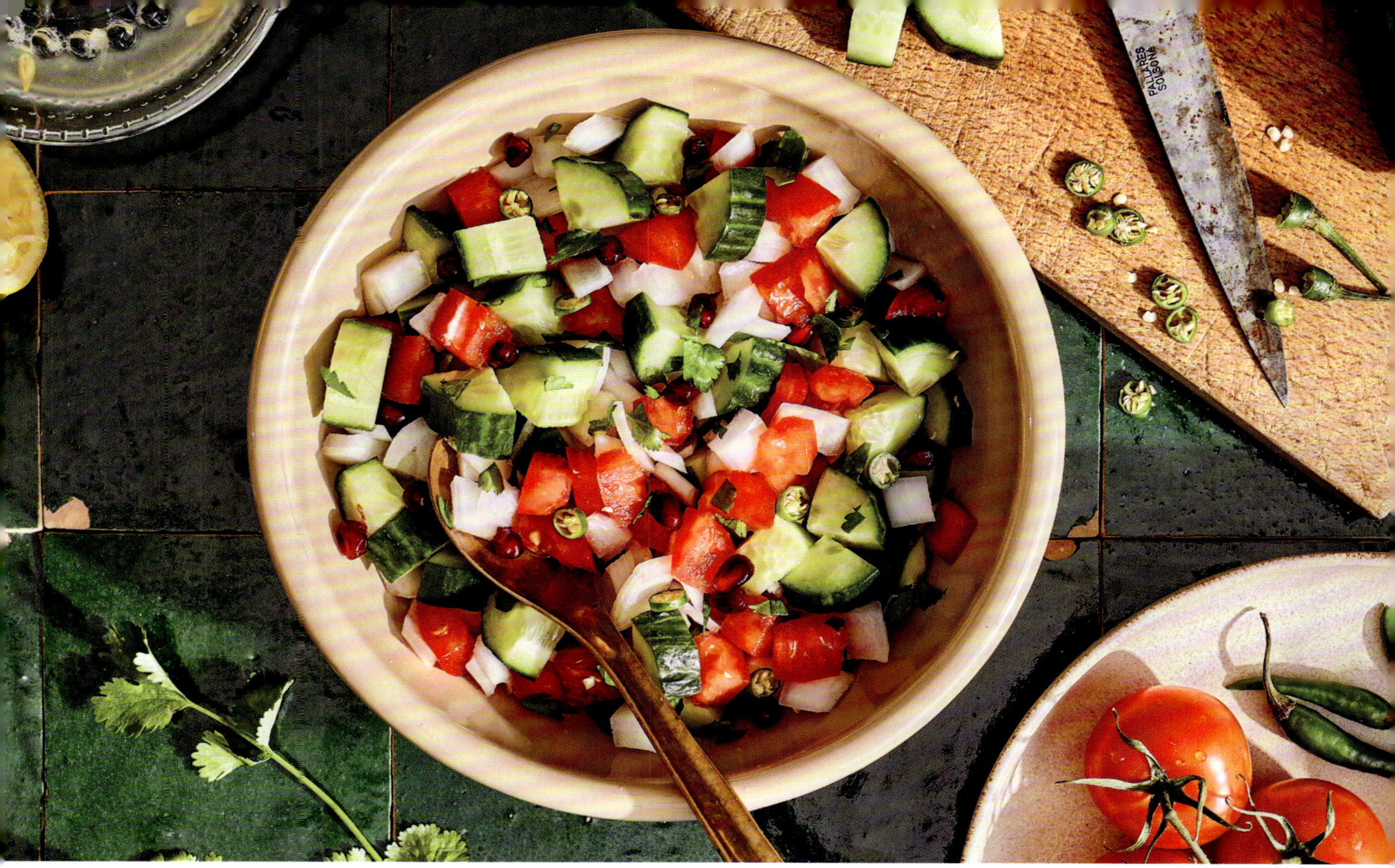

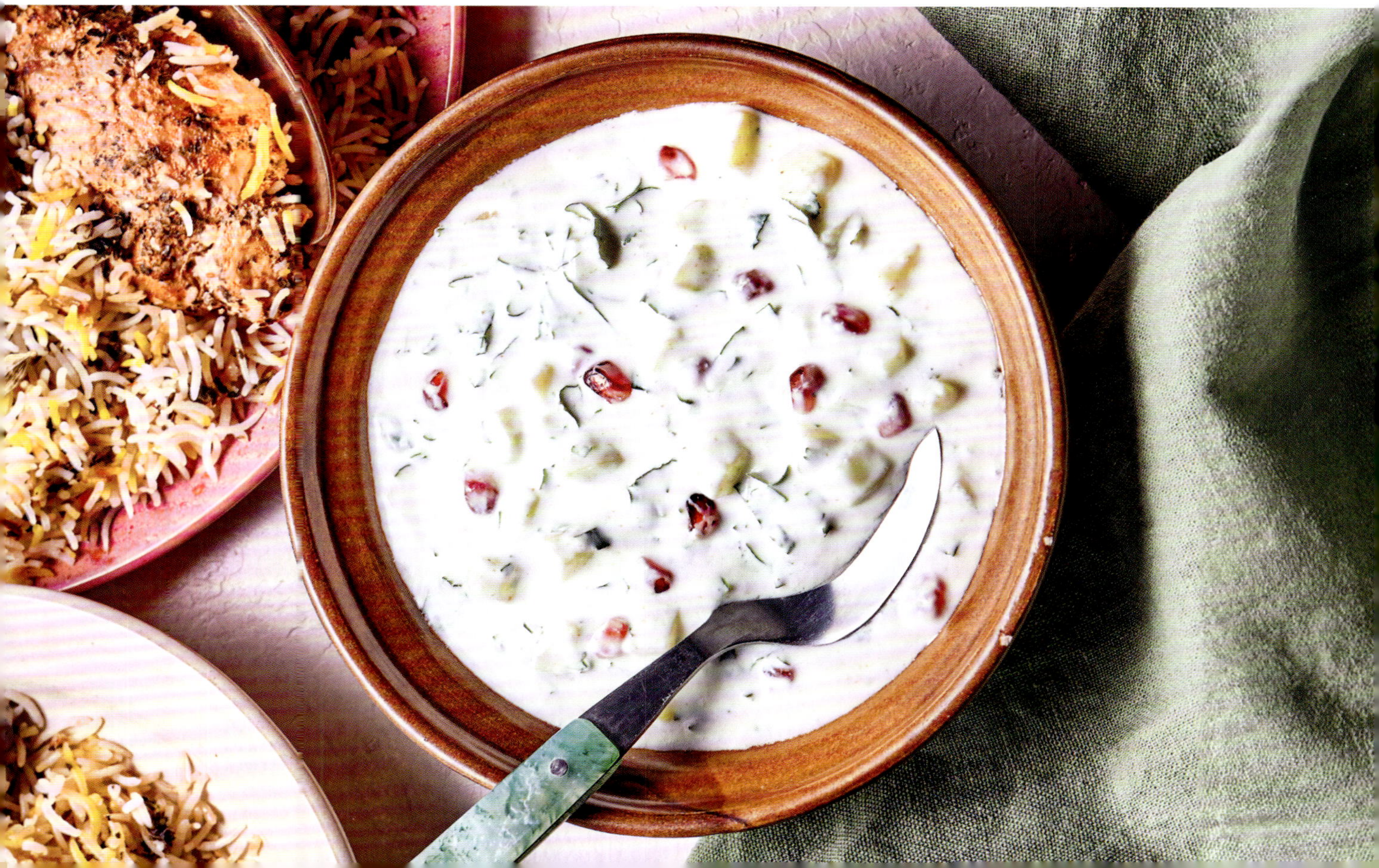

4-Ingredient Tamarind Chutney

MAKES 1½ CUPS

¼ cup seedless tamarind pulp

1½ cups boiling water, divided

1 cup finely chopped or powdered jaggery or ¾ cup brown sugar

3 tsp ground cumin

2 tsp Kashmiri chili powder

Kosher salt

Sweet, tangy, savory, and spicy, this tamarind chutney is used as an accompaniment for many Indian snack dishes, including Easy Mixed Vegetable Samosas (page 21) and Crispy Onion and Jalapeño Pakodas (page 26). The use of a blender makes the preparation of this chutney super simple.

Add the tamarind to a small bowl and top with ½ cup of the boiling water. Soak for 20 minutes. Transfer to a blender and blend until smooth. Add the remaining 1 cup boiling water and blend again. Strain the mixture into a bowl through a fine mesh sieve, discarding any pulp or fibers left behind.

Transfer the strained tamarind juice to a small saucepan and add the jaggery, cumin, chili powder, and salt to taste. Bring to a simmer and cook for 10 to 12 minutes or until the chutney takes on a deep brown color and thickens slightly. Transfer to a container and cool completely.

Serve with your favorite Indian snacks or appetizers. Store in an airtight container in the fridge for up to a month.

5-Minute Coconut Chutney

MAKES 1½ CUPS

1 cup fresh grated coconut
 (or frozen that has been thawed)

¼ cup raw cashews

2 slices ginger, each ⅜ inch
 (1 cm) thick

2 Thai green chilis

¾ cup warm water

Kosher salt

2 Tbsp canola oil

1 tsp black mustard seeds

1 tsp skinless urad dhal (black gram)

10 fresh curry leaves

Creamy coconut chutney is a popular condiment from South India that is served as an accompaniment to several dishes, including 4-Ingredient Dosas (page 175), 5-Ingredient Masala Vada (page 39), and 20-Minute Vegetable Upma (page 149). Make the chutney just before serving for the best texture and flavor.

Add the coconut, cashews, ginger, chilis, and water to a blender, and season with salt to taste. Blend until smooth.

Heat a small frying pan on medium-high and add the oil. Once hot, add the mustard seeds, and let them pop for a few seconds. Add the urad dhal and toast for 20 seconds or until just golden. Lastly, tear the curry leaves and add them to the hot oil. Immediately pour the hot spiced oil over the chutney. Stir to combine.

Store in an airtight container in the fridge for up to 1 day. If the chutney thickens in the fridge, stir in a bit of warm water to return to creamy consistency.

Green Mango with Chili Salt

SERVES 2

1 large green mango
 (see note on page 227)

1 Tbsp kosher salt

1 Tbsp cayenne chili powder

Visits to Marina Beach while on vacation in Chennai always included stopping at vendors selling freshly cut green mango with chili and salt. The crunch of the sour mango paired with the hot chili and salt was an addictive combination that we could never resist. While I do love eating it on its own as a snack, it is also a great side dish to serve with Indian dishes like curd rice (see Thayir Sadam, page 141).

Slice along the seed of the mango to separate the flesh, then cut each mango half into long ½-inch-wide (1.5 cm) strips. Using a paring knife, cut many slits along the flesh of the mango, ensuring not to cut through the skin. This will give a fan-like appearance to the mango strips.

Mix the salt and chili powder in a small bowl. Sprinkle the chili salt all over the mango and serve immediately (this doesn't store well for later).

Coriander Lime Mayo

MAKES 1 CUP

1 cup mayonnaise

½ cup fresh coriander (cilantro)

3 Thai green chilis

1 tsp ground cumin

1 clove garlic, finely grated

Juice and zest of 1 lime

Kosher salt

From French fries, to burgers, to chicken tenders, this spicy and tangy coriander lime mayo is great on a lot of things! I love serving it as a dipping sauce with the Curry Popcorn Shrimp (page 35).

Add the mayonnaise, fresh coriander, chilis, cumin, garlic, and lime juice and zest to a small blender. Season with salt to taste, and blend until smooth.

Store in an airtight container in the fridge for up to 1 week.

Mint Coriander Chutney

MAKES 1½ CUPS

1 cup fresh coriander (cilantro)

1 cup fresh mint leaves

¾ cup chopped sweet white onion

4 Thai green chilis

Juice of 1 lemon

Kosher salt

Fragrant and zippy, mint coriander chutney is a staple in Indian cuisine. Great with Easy Mixed Vegetable Samosas (page 21), Crispy Onion and Jalapeño Pakodas (page 26), and Cheesy Keema Quesadillas (page 128), the freshness of the herbs and tang of the lemon in this chutney really elevate and perk up the flavor of these dishes effortlessly.

Add the fresh coriander, mint, onion, chilis, and lemon juice to a small blender. Season with salt to taste. Blend until smooth.

Store in an airtight container in the fridge for up to 1 week.

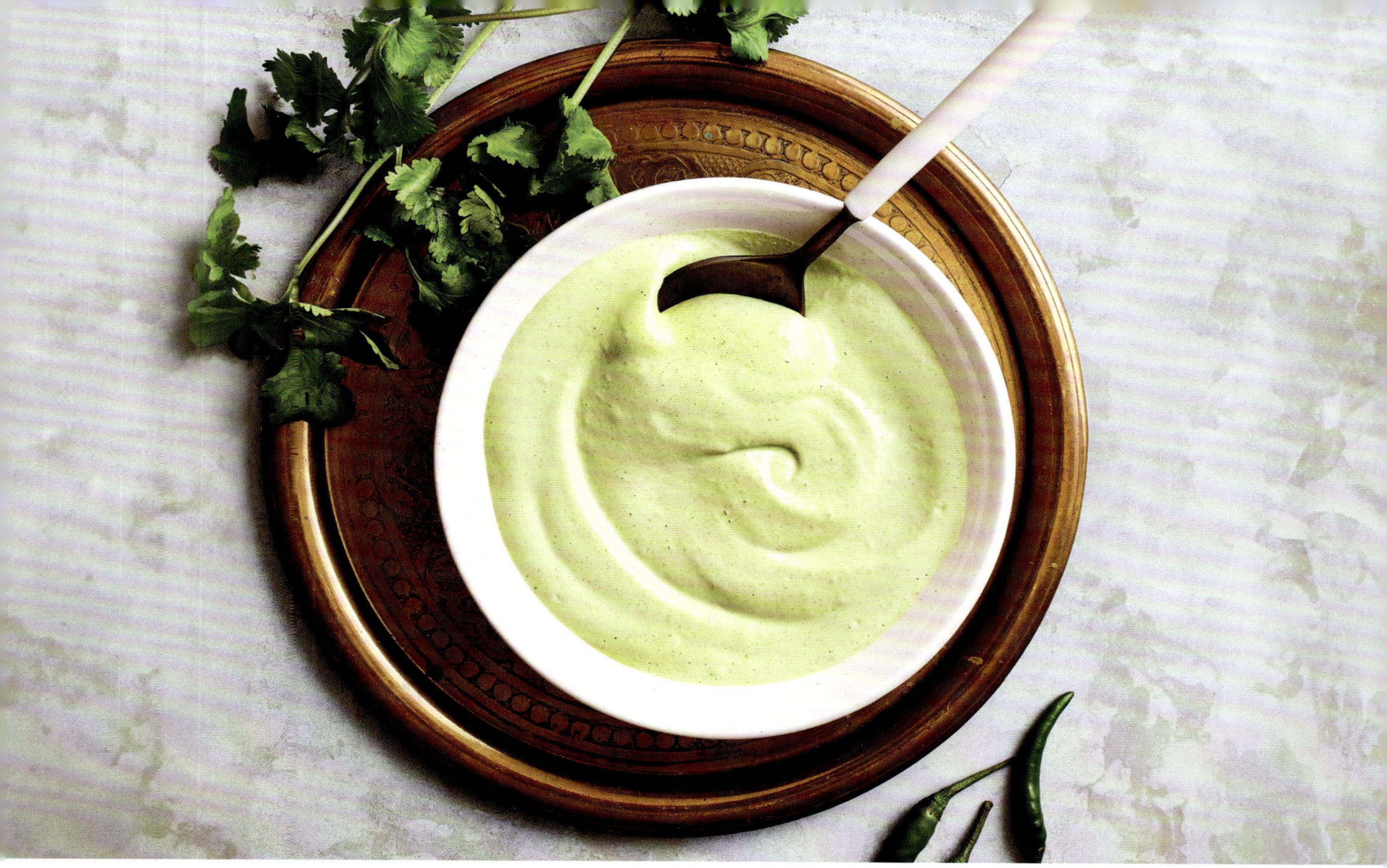

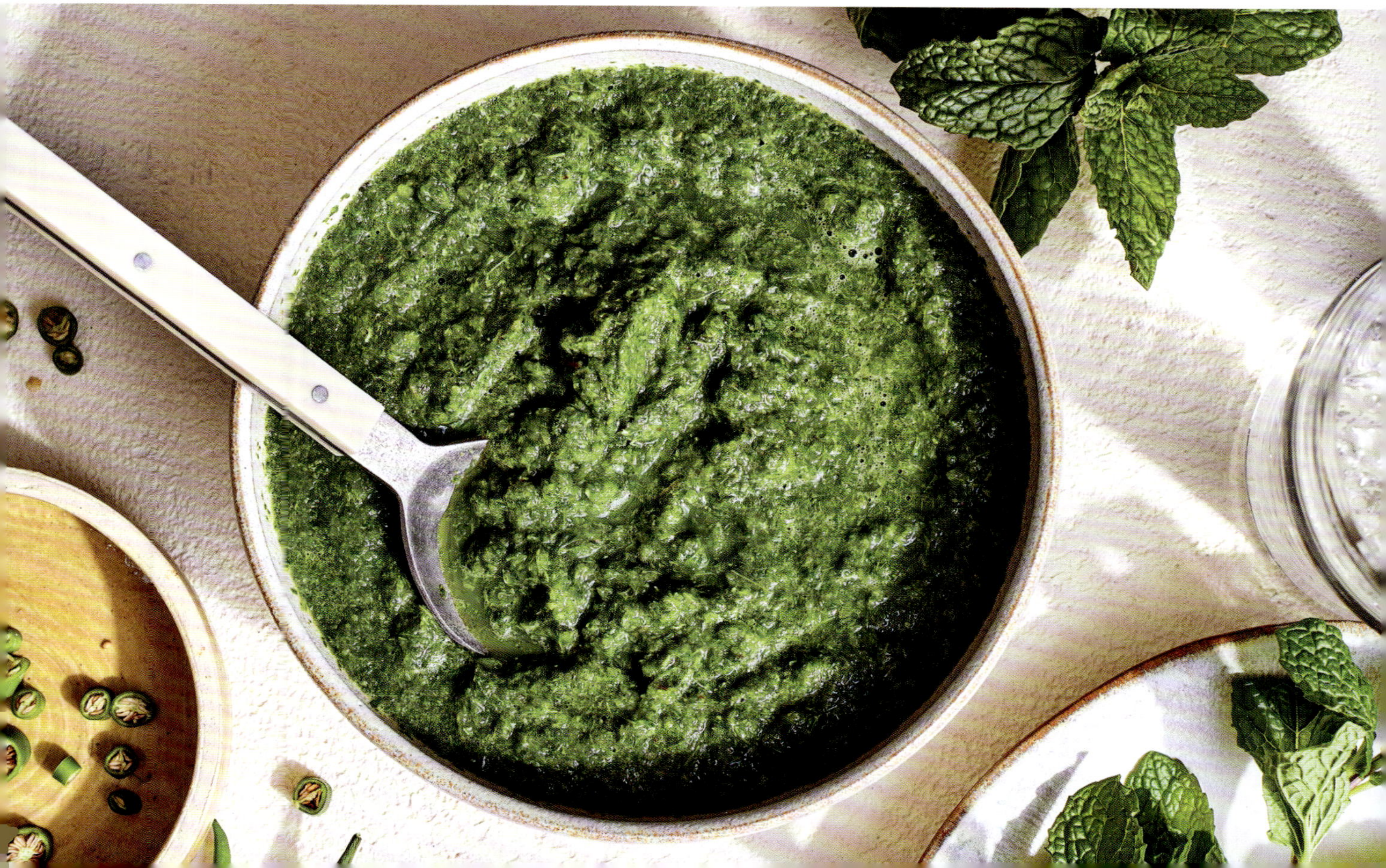

2-Ingredient Onion Pachadi

MAKES 3 CUPS

2 cups plain yogurt

1 medium sweet onion, thinly sliced

Kosher salt

Whenever biryani is served in our family, there is always a big bowl of onion pachadi on the side. The crunch of the sweet onions combined with the creamy, tangy yogurt go so well together with a hot plate of South Indian Lamb Biryani (page 153). It is not to be missed!

Add the yogurt and sliced onion to a bowl and season with salt to taste. Mix to combine.

Store in an airtight container in the fridge for up to 2 days.

Garam Masala

MAKES ¼ CUP

2 Tbsp coriander seeds

2 Tbsp cumin seeds

6 green cardamom pods

6 cloves

1 cinnamon stick

¼ whole nutmeg

1 star anise

1 tsp black peppercorns

While garam masala is now widely available at grocery stores, I do recommend making it at home for several reasons. First, making it in small batches ensures that it's super fresh and aromatic. Second, once you familiarize yourself with this recipe, you can tinker with the quantity and variety of spices to create your own house blend.

Add the coriander seeds, cumin seeds, cardamom pods, cloves, cinnamon, nutmeg, star anise, and peppercorns to a coffee grinder or small Indian mixer grinder jar. Grind until the mixture forms a fine powder.

Store in a sealed jar in your pantry for up to 3 months.

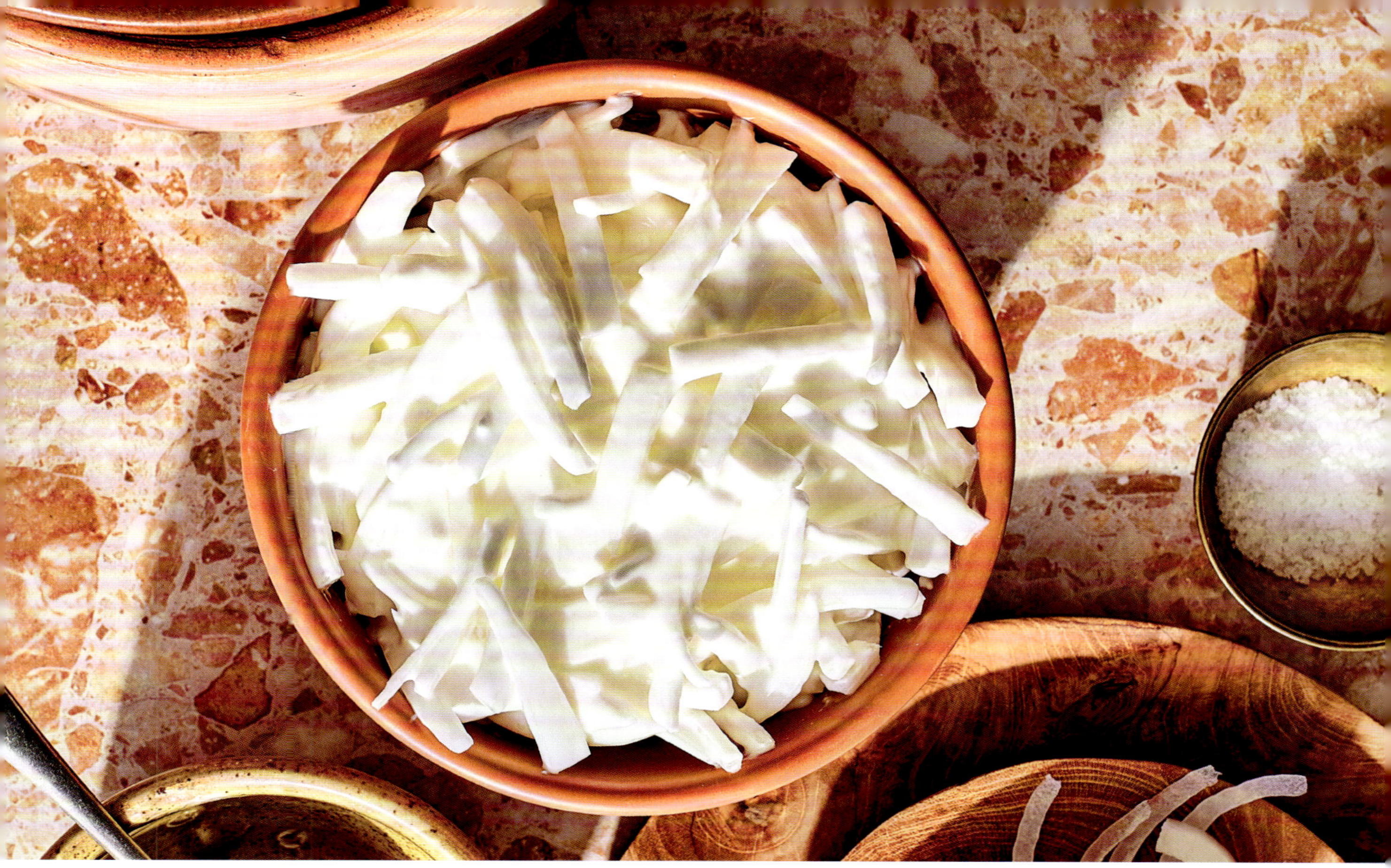
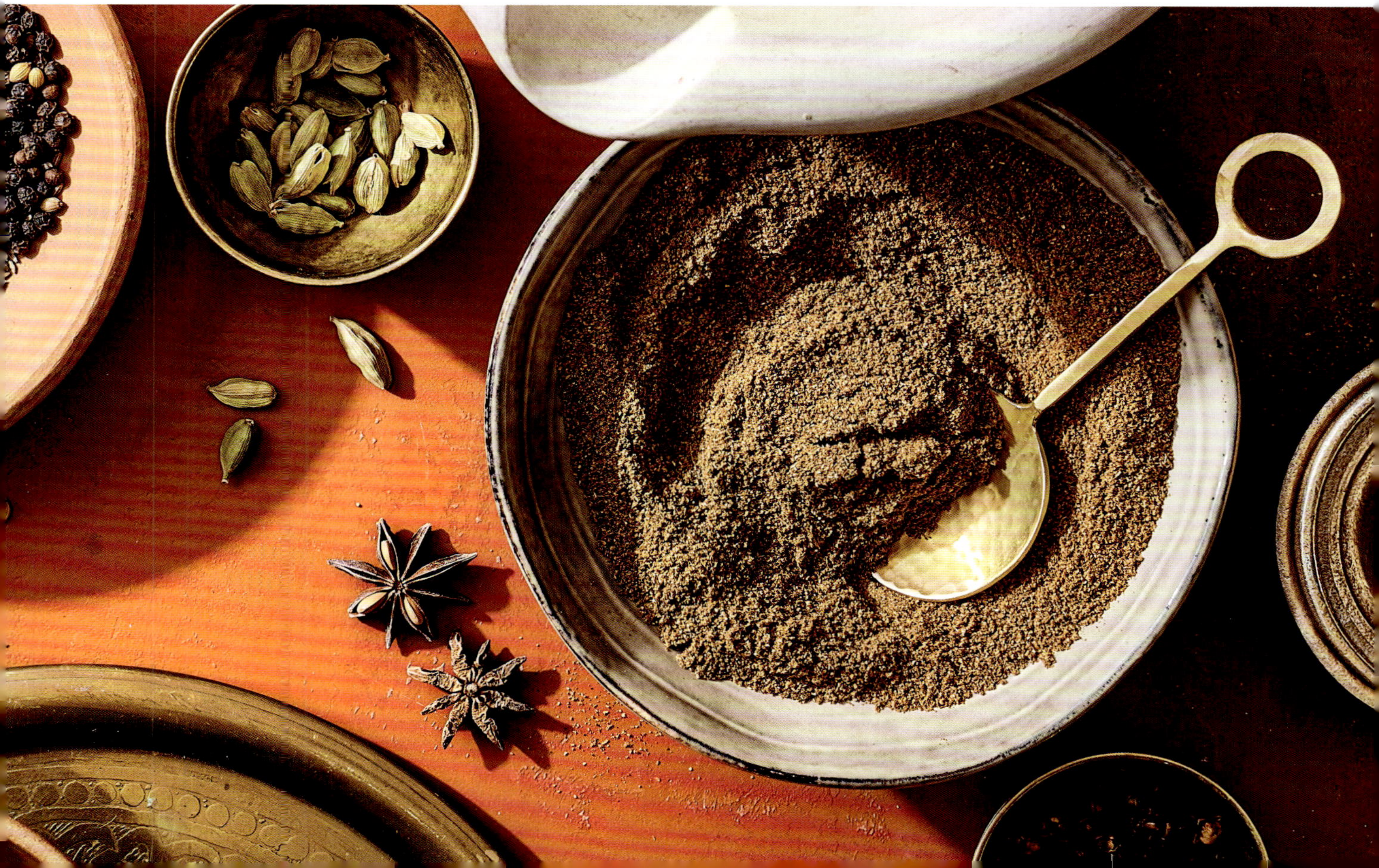

Acknowledgments

When I was six years old and began watching cooking shows for the first time, I never imagined that one day I would write a cookbook of my own. I am incredibly grateful for this opportunity, and to little Vijaya for talking to herself in the mirror, any chance she got, pretending to be a cooking show host. She manifested this!

To every culinary legend I've watched on TV, thank you for inspiring me! From Madhur Jaffrey to Emeril Lagasse to Jamie Oliver, you were my stars, and you ignited my passion for cooking and made me believe that I too could teach others through the wonderful media of television and literature.

To my mom, my greatest supporter from day one, thank you for always believing in me and giving me all the encouragement to pursue what many would consider an "out there" career. You have passed down so much wisdom to me and shared your greatest culinary secrets with patience, and for that I am forever grateful.

My deepest appreciation goes to my husband, who has been my sounding board through the entire book-writing process. He saw me through every wave of emotion and kept me grounded each step of the way. I am so lucky to have him as my partner and greatest cheerleader in life. Also, his attention to detail is unparalleled! He is simply the best!

To my children, thank you for being ever so patient, and for enthusiastically trying everything Mama cooks. You are the most precious sweet peas, and I am so lucky to cook with you and for you every day.

I am also immensely thankful to my publisher, Appetite by Random House, for believing in me and the concept for this book. A huge thank you to Robert McCullough and to my incredible editor, Rachel Brown, for their unwavering support and dedication throughout what has been one of the biggest projects of my life.

To my wonderful photographer, Tanya Pilgrim, and food stylist, Julya Hajnoczky, thank you for bringing my food to life through your beautiful styling and imagery. Indian food has never looked more beautiful!

Last but not least, my heartfelt gratitude to you, the reader, for picking this book up and adding it to your repertoire! I am incredibly honored that you have chosen me to guide you through the world of Indian cuisine and am thrilled that you will be trying some of my most cherished recipes.

All my love,
Vijaya

Index